OP 91-
1250

Suicide and Despair in
the Jacobean Drama

Suicide and Despair in the Jacobean Drama

Rowland Wymer

Lecturer in English
University of Hull

ST. MARTIN'S PRESS   NEW YORK

ISBN 0-312-77526-1

Library of Congress Cataloging-in-Publication Data

Wymer, Rowland
  Suicide and despair in the Jacobean drama.

  Revision of thesis (M.Litt.)—Oxford.
  Bibliography: p.
  Includes index.
  1. English drama—17th century—History and criticism   2.
English drama (Tragedy)—History and criticism.   3. Shakespeare,
William, 1564-1615—Tragedies.   4. Suicide in literature.   5.
Despair in literature.   I. Title.
PR658.T7W9   1985   822'3'09353   85-22111
ISBN 0-312-77526-1

In memory of my father,
who gave me so many books

yet is every man his greatest enemy, and as it were, his owne executioner ... for I perceive every man is his owne *Atropos*, and lends a hand to cut the thred of his owne days.

(Sir Thomas Browne, *Religio Medici*)

Contents

Preface

This study of suicide in the plays of Shakespeare and his contemporaries had its origin in a strong conviction that the topic epitomised many of the central conflicts in Renaissance thought, and hence had an especially expressive value for Renaissance dramatists. The culturally problematic status of suicide and its relation to despair provided inexhaustible opportunities for writers wishing to generate different kinds of ethical complication and emotional effect. All the tragic playwrights of this period show some awareness of the artistic usefulness of suicide and so, by covering a large number of plays, I have tried to give a full sense of how certain powerful moments in some of the greatest plays of the period have been developed out of a commonly-held set of conventions and assumptions. Inevitably, perhaps, it is Shakespeare who appears most alert to the many different dramatic nuances of suicide, and the majority of chapters culminate in analyses of his plays. The light thrown on aspects of *Hamlet*, *Macbeth*, *Lear*, *Othello*, *Antony and Cleopatra*, and *Julius Caesar*, together with Webster's *Duchess of Malfi*, is, I hope, one of the ways in which my whole endeavour has justified itself.

As will already be apparent, my general approach is a historical and intentionalist one. The major categories I have employed are those of the period itself, and I have been more interested in discussing the way writers *intentionally* manipulated some of the contradictions of their culture for calculated dramatic effects, than in viewing the plays primarily as sociological documents which *involuntarily* reveal contradictions in the social formation. The most powerful theoretical arguments justifying such a traditional critical approach are to be found in the writings of E. D. Hirsch, Jr, namely *Validity in Interpretation* (Yale University Press: New Haven and London, 1967) and *The Aims of*

Interpretation (University of Chicago Press: Chicago and London, 1976), to which I refer any reader who is convinced that the author is now safely dead. A further important influence was Norman Rabkin's *Shakespeare and the Common Understanding* (The Free Press: New York/Collier-Macmillan: London, 1967), because of its persuasive explanation of major literature's power over us in terms of its dualistic presentation of kinds of conflict which elude logical resolution. The question of suicide, despite major changes in social attitudes, continues to raise fundamental issues of a kind which are extremely difficult to resolve, and remains the type of subject to which literature is particularly drawn and with which, perhaps, it is particularly well equipped to deal.

For my purposes, the 'Jacobean' phase of the drama may be said to begin just before 1600, with the appearance of Shakespeare's *Julius Caesar* and Marston's *Antonio and Mellida*. However, I have not hesitated to quote extensively from earlier plays when, as in the cases of *Doctor Faustus* and *Romeo and Juliet*, they are especially relevant to my argument. I have taken 1625 as a terminal date, but have discussed later works by Ford and Massinger, whose careers were established during the Jacobean period proper. Closet dramas of whatever date have been excluded from consideration.

Information on the dating and authorship of plays discussed is based on Alfred Harbage's *Annals of English Drama* as revised by S. Schoenbaum (1964), occasionally supplemented by reference to other authorities. The editions used for quotations from plays are listed in a separate part of the Bibliography. When the preferred edition has no line-numbering, the page number and, where appropriate, the volume number is given instead. In the case of Beaumont and Fletcher, those plays which do not appear in the first five volumes of the Bowers edition have the abbreviation 'Cam.' (signifying the Cambridge edition of Glover and Waller) included in quotation references. In all plays, whenever passages of dialogue are quoted, the speech prefixes have been expanded and normalised. In old-spelling quotations, 'u', 'v', 'i', 'j' and long 's' have been given in their modern form. Biblical quotations are from the Authorised Version.

This book began life as an Oxford M.Litt. thesis and I would like to thank Dame Helen Gardner, John Carey, and Emrys

Jones for the encouragement and advice they gave at that stage of its development. Since then I have been grateful to Harriet Hawkins and, especially, Tom McAlindon for further useful suggestions. My thanks also to Sue Beales for her typing, and to Bridget Atkinson for some different perspectives on suicide.

CHAPTER 1

Suicide, Despair, and the Drama

> And tragical, my noble lord, it is,
> For Pyramus therein doth kill himself.
> (Shakespeare)

I

In Antony Copley's allegorical poem *A Fig for Fortune*, printed in 1596, '*An* Elizian *out-cast of Fortune, ranging on his Jade* Melancholie *through the Desert of his affliction*' meets the ghost of Cato, '*a spirit of Dispair & self-misdoom*', which tempts him to kill himself. The descripton of Cato's ghost is modelled on traditional representations of the nature of man—half-beast and half-angel:

> His upper shape was faire-Angelicall,
> The rest belowe, all whollie Serpentine,
> Cole-blacke incroching upon his pectorall,
> And rudely inrowlled in a Gorgon-twine.[1]

Like man, suicide had a double nature whose contradictory aspects could never be wholly reconciled.

During the Elizabethan and Jacobean period, the Christian view of suicide as the product and symbol of a damnable despair was still dominant, but was beginning to be challenged. Throughout the Middle Ages theological condemnation of suicide had coexisted with favourable literary treatment of it in certain circumstances, particularly when undertaken for love or in defence of female chastity. The emphasis on personal honour in the chivalric code had also produced an attitude which saw death as sometimes preferable to shame for a knight. All these

1

traditions were carried through into the Renaissance along with the Christian teaching with which they were often at variance: 'For the aristocratic military class there is direct continuity of cultural ideals from the late Romans and Teutons, through the Middle Ages, to the Renaissance.'[2] But it was only in the Renaissance that secular ideas of honour were formally developed and propagated in a way which brought them into direct philosophical conflict with Christianity. Contradictions which had coexisted peacefully for hundreds of years, owing to the medieval capacity for a kind of doublethink, were activated by the humanists' intensive study of Roman history and Roman ideas. Classical notions of honour with their non-Christian emphasis on 'reputation' were adopted and systematised in works of moral philosophy. The lives and deaths of the heroes of antiquity were scrutinised with a new thoroughness in the search for valid ideals of human conduct.

One consequence of this new historical perspective was a re-examination of the ethics of suicide, the sinfulness of which had remained unquestioned in medieval theology and philosophy. Renaissance discussion of famous classical suicides such as Cato and Lucrece opened out inevitably into wide-ranging moral debates. On the Continent, Montaigne and Charron removed many of the supposedly 'rational' objections to suicide and, in England, John Donne wrote *Biathanatos*, 'A Declaration of that Paradox or Thesis, that Self-Homicide is not so naturally Sin that it may never be otherwise'.[3] The word 'suicide' itself, latinate and morally neutral, is a product of the new outlook. The first known use of the word is in Sir Thomas Browne's *Religio Medici* (Part I, sect. 44), written in 1635, and published in 1642. Unlike the older terms, 'self-murder' and 'self-slaughter', it avoids the implication of violence and criminality.[4] However, in orthodox theology suicide remained firmly associated with final despair—'the damnablest thing that may be by the rules of the Christen religion'[5]—and even in the writings of Montaigne and Charron a continual wavering between the Christian and classical viewpoints is discernible.

The Jacobean drama was written and performed at a time when suicide was reacquiring the dignity and honour of its Roman past, but had not lost its medieval connotations of shame and despair. The more problematic it was for moralists, the more useful it was to writers of literature looking for a pointed expression of the ambiguities they perceived in human nature and human conduct. An early example of the literary value of suicide's equivocal moral status is the Earl of Surrey's sonnet on the Assyrian king, Sardanapalus, which attacks him as a degenerate, 'effeminate' ruler. The sonnet concludes as follows:

> Who scace the name of manhode dyd retayne,
> Drenched in slouthe and womanishe delight,
> Feble of sprete, unpacyent of payne,
> When he hadd lost his honor and hys right,
>   Prowde tyme of welthe, in stormes appawld with drede,
>   Murdered hym selfe to shew some manfull dede.[6]

The epigrammatic wit and force of that last line depends entirely on the reader being able to think of suicide as both an act of cowardice and an act of heroism, the final proof of the king's effeminacy or his only manly action. Prior to the great period of the drama, the most thoroughgoing literary exploitation of suicide's multiple significance occurs in Sidney's *Arcadia*, where a whole range of different contexts and motivations is created, forcing the reader into complex comparisons and judgements.[7] Sidney's engagement with the topic is enlivened by his sense of its many paradoxes. When Pyrocles threatens to kill himself to safeguard Philoclea's reputation, she employs most of the standard moral arguments against suicide in order to dissuade him, but the only argument which works is a threat to kill herself as well if he goes ahead with his decision. Ethical absolutes give way to emotional realities, as so often in *Arcadia*.

But it was the theatre, the age's major art-form, which benefited most from the different ways in which suicide could be viewed. The typical Roman suicide was an act of deliberate, self-conscious nobility which already carried strong suggestions of theatricality. Once knowledge of the classical past became widespread, playwrights inevitably became eager to make use of its theatrical potential. Such suicides—along with deaths for love or chastity which literature had already, in part, rescued from the dictates of theology—supplemented rather than supplanted the idea of suicide as an act of despair which was part of the drama's medieval heritage, and had been given extensive dramatic expression in the Morality plays. The Jacobean drama was indebted both directly and indirectly to medieval traditions of suicide and despair; directly because, 'In spite of the tides of secularism, despair in its theological sense—loss of hope of salvation—figures significantly in Renaissance literature.'[8] A less direct but still important debt concerns the way mental torment of a non-religious kind was portrayed in tragic drama, for 'the despair topos, like others originally theological in nature, passed over into secular literature.'[9]

In fact, the two faces of suicide—dignity and despair—could be said to comprise an important part of the paradoxical effect of tragedy just as they encompass the Renaissance view of man as 'a proud and yet a wretched thing'. All important theories of tragedy from Hegel onwards have stressed the importance of conflict and contradiction in achieving the tragic effect: 'From the beginning, in all discussions of tragedy, one note is struck: that tragedy includes, or reconciles, or preserves in tension, contraries.'[10] More specifically, much of the best criticism of Shakespeare in recent years has emphasised the dualistic, paradoxical quality of his vision and his art: 'For Shakespeare... paradox is a concise embodiment of the tragic fact—a specific and radical observation about the workings of nature.'[11] Although it is becoming more and more apparent that the dialectical approach taken by Shakespeare and some of his contemporaries to every topic is something which is deeply rooted in Renaissance habits of thought,[12] it is probably the single most important reason that their art remains so strongly alive for us today. The truth of their mimesis lies, for us, in its powerful enactment of dynamic contradictions.

In tragedy, the sense of paradox is often particularly sharp and the action organised in a way which brings into conflict a whole series of polarities. One of the most important of these is the way that a terrible sense of suffering, failure, and despair is often combined with an assertion of human dignity in the face of death. Both these elements of tragedy could be, and often were, aptly symbolised by a character's suicide. As J.M.R. Margeson points out,[13] early plays like *Apius and Virginia* and *Soliman and Perseda* tend to express this duality in the simplest possible manner. The threatened virgin kills herself with honour, while the lustful tyrant dies in despair. In the greatest tragedies of the Jacobean period the divisions between the suicidal 'types' break down and a more truly tragic, paradoxically mixed response is evoked. The gradual decline of the drama in the later years of James's reign brought about a reversion to the crude typecasting of the Elizabethan period. In the plays of Fletcher and his collaborators, the differing implications of suicide are often discussed, but our response to any particular suicide is usually uncomplicated, and governed largely by the stock type the character represents, whether virgin, noble Roman, atheist, or tyrant. The many 'noble' offers of death made in these plays as a means of argument and persuasion ('Rip up this bosom, and pluck out the heart') are the logical culmination of a simplistic use of the implications of suicide. What was potentially the supreme tragic act has dwindled to a rhetorical gesture.

I have been suggesting that the most interesting and fully dramatic uses of suicide depend on an awareness of its double nature and an exploitation of the Renaissance tendency to conflate Christian and classical traditions. This is a part of the truth, but not all of it. Independent of any particular historical tradition, the inherently contradictory nature of an act which is both self-assertive and self-cancelling has the dramatic advantage of condensing psychological and thematic conflicts into a single spectacular gesture. Moreover, what needs to be added is that Christian thought on suicide and despair contained, within itself, sufficient paradox to produce dramatic tension and a tragic complexity. Although suicide, in whatever circumstances, was believed to signify damnation, the martyrs of the early Church had often died in ways which bordered on suicide. For instance, Apollonia, after being tortured, had thrown herself into the fire prepared for her, 'being inflamed with a more burning fire of the Holy Ghost'.[14] The very basis of Christianity, the death of Jesus, could be regarded as a form of suicide[15] and was sometimes emblematised by the pelican, which was believed to pierce its own breast in order to nourish its young with its life-blood.[16] The combined effect of Donne's *Biathanatos* and *Pseudo-Martyr*, written within a year or two of each other, is to challenge the way the distinction between suicide and martyrdom was often made. According to Donne, if the intentions of the person involved were considered carefully, many deaths which had been recorded as suicides should be classified as martyrdoms, and vice versa. Sir

Thomas More himself, to whom Donne was related on his mother's side, had been strongly aware of the spiritual dangers of an actively sought martyrdom.[17] All in all, voluntary death had a more equivocal status in Christian thought than many theologians were prepared to admit.

Still more interesting are the paradoxes at the heart of Christian doctrine concerning despair. Although despair was above all sins the 'sinne most displesant to Crist, and most adversarie',[18] it was also closely associated with redemption. The sorrow for sin (*tristitia*) which could bring a person to despair was also a necessary first step to achieving a state of grace. The dagger clutched by a personified Despair in the Morality plays had implicit and paradoxical connections with the lance used by Penance to touch the heart of Mankind with contrition. In the suicide of Othello the dramatic possibilities of such connections were fulfilled. The Reformation increased the importance placed on the positive side of despair. In Lutheran theology, a conviction of one's own worthlessness, an absolute self-despair, was the necessary prelude to a complete reliance on God's grace. Luther reached his idea of justification by faith alone by passing through such a period of despair, which was why he could later say 'how beautiful that despair was, and how near to Grace'.[19] For those who followed Luther's teaching it became a spiritual necessity to undergo this kind of self-despair. Without such an experience of worthlessness, one might be tempted to question God's justice.

> For except thou have born the cross of adversity and temptation, and hast felt thyself brought unto the very brim of desperation, yea, and unto hell-gates, thou canst never meddle with the sentence of predestination without thine own harm, and without secret wrath and grudging inwardly against God; for otherwise it shall not be possible for thee to think that God is righteous and just.[20]

As with the problem of suicide and martyrdom, there was, in theory, a clear distinction between this saving kind of self-despair and the damning despair of God's mercy, 'the one a wicked kind of Desperation of Gods promises, power, goodness, & mercie towards sinners... The other an holy Desperation of a mans owne defectes, infirmities, and corruptions.'[21] St Paul's contrast between 'godly sorrow' and 'sorrow of the world' was often cited in this context.[22] Since, however, despair over one's own wickedness could involve a sense of being cut off from God, such a distinction was often clearer in theory than in practice. Similarly, the other type of theological distinction usually made—between temporal despair which 'may befal the best of God's children' and final despair—seems to be based not on any real difference in the nature of the spiritual anguish endured, but on whether such a state continues till the moment of death. Christ's terrible cry on the cross, 'My God, my God, why hast thou forsaken me?', was of course classified as temporal despair, yet it has all the force of a complete and final loss of hope. The intensity of the torment was no guide to whether an individual's despair was a mark of damnation or, like other kinds of affliction, a necessary stage in the achievement of grace.

The secularisation of the drama led not only to the free depiction of honourable suicides, but also to a reworking, in more secular terms, of the frequently ambivalent Christian notions concerning despair and suicide. Although the Elizabethan and Jacobean tragic *form* was mainly a matter of ending a play with deaths—suicides of whatever nature being one way of accomplishing this—the greatest achievements of the age in tragedy involve the idea of despair, whether in its original and specifically religious sense or in its later and broader application. As Lily B. Campbell wrote,

> Death itself is not so terrible as the loss of will to live which we see in each of the great tragic heroes of Shakespeare... It is not the death of Hamlet or Othello or Macbeth or Lear that awes and horrifies us but the despair and disillusion that grows within his soul as he views the desolation and confusion to which he has contributed.[23]

It is not surprising that the first Elizabethan play to touch the note of true tragedy, Marlowe's *Doctor Faustus*, should be a classic study of religious despair. Christianity, with its message of hope for mankind in general, is less inimical to tragedy than is often claimed. For the individual who has lost that hope, and the movement of the drama was from the general to the individual case—from Mankind and Everyman to Faustus and Macbeth—there is a despair that can be fully tragic. Our response to the last Act of *Doctor Faustus* is the same as our response to the great Jacobean tragedies. 'Marlowe, the leader of the earlier age in tragic thought, already points it towards the sense of defeat that was so marked a characteristic of the Jacobeans.'[24] In this context it is interesting to note that John Vyvyan, in *The Shakespearean Ethic*, considered that the life of Judas Iscariot, the archetype of suicidal despair, 'might have been Shakespeare's paradigm of tragedy'.[25]

In the preceding pages, I have tried to indicate the main areas of concern in this book. These may be summarised as follows: a convergence of differing religious, philosophical, and literary traditions at the Renaissance meant that a stage suicide could evoke whatever response a dramatist wished. The shifting relationship of suicide and despair in the Jacobean drama represents, on the whole, a pragmatic rather than a moralistic use by the individual playwrights of an almost infinitely flexible dramatic convention. Although frequently useful as an image of criminal despair on the one hand, or transcendent nobility on the other, the most interesting treatments of suicide involve either a tension between what might be called the positive and negative implications of the act, or else an exploitation of the paradoxes that constitute the darker face of suicide—despair. The remainder of this chapter will consist of a short history of Western attitudes to suicide—the differing traditions which underlie the varied use of suicide in the drama—up to and including the Jacobean period; an account of the theological and artistic association of suicide with despair, together with some remarks on the changing significance of despair; and finally a comparison of some of the ways in which playwrights expressed the double nature of suicide. Before concluding this section, however, I should like to re-emphasise the importance of suicide as a touchstone of character in the drama, and its peculiar aptness as an image for the human condition as commonly conceived in this period.

Both Christian and classical thought stressed the great significance of the manner of a person's death, though from rather different standpoints. Montaigne had the Stoic ideal of a quiet and constant death in mind when he wrote, 'When I judge of other men's lives, I ever respect how they have behaved themselves in their end.'[26] For a more orthodox Christian, the significance would lie less in the dignity and assurance with which death was met, than in the possibility of a last-minute repentance. Both Catholics and moderate Anglicans believed that a saving repentance could come between the bridge and the brook, the stirrup and the ground, 'for God judge[s] every one as his end is, and not as his life was'.[27] In these circumstances, it is not surprising that the dramatists should adopt 'the romantic convention, that men are, in the second of death, most essentially and significantly themselves.'[28] As Montaigne put it, translating Lucretius,

> For then are sent true speeches from the heart,
> We are ourselves, we leave to play a part.[29]

Not every writer on the Renaissance shares Montaigne's confidence that the moment of death is one of authentic self-revelation. Instead, some choose to emphasise the theatricality with which many of the period's great men and women faced their deaths:

> The truly memorable death scenes of the age, on the scaffold, at home, or even on the battlefield—Sir Thomas More, Mary Queen of Scots, Sir Philip Sidney, John Donne, Ralegh, Charles I—were precisely that: *scenes*, presided over by actor-playwrights who had brilliantly conceived and thoroughly mastered their roles.[30]

But in a stage suicide, of course, an interplay of sincerity and theatricality may be an important part of the dramatist's conception of a character. The many connotations suicide possessed for the Renaissance meant that only lack of skill could prevent a playwright fashioning a death in every way appropriate to the character concerned, even to the extent of expressing a tendency to self-dramatisation.

In more general terms, suicide can be regarded as epitomising the tragic view of man as a uniquely divided and self-destructive being. Despite the emblematic myth of the pelican, it was generally accepted that man was the only creature who was capable of killing himself:

> which practise of *self-murder* all other creatures doe abhorre, by

the instinct of *nature*: *and* so we see, that the most *noble* creatures are obnoxious [i.e. liable] and subject to commit the greatest errors, by their abuse of their most eminent parts.[31]

Every quality that helps to raise man above the beasts can also be the means by which he destroys himself:

> We have not any strength but weakens us,
> No greatness but doth crush us into air.[32]

This idea is implicit in all the great Jacobean tragedies, as is the similar intuition of Robert Burton that 'every man' is 'the greatest enemy unto himself'.[33] The act of suicide was an especially apt symbol for such perceptions. Ferdinand's remark at the end of *The Duchess of Malfi*,

> *Whether we fall by ambition, blood, or lust,*
> *Like diamonds, we are cut with our own dust.*
> (V.v. 72–3)

can be figuratively applied to the entire body of Jacobean tragedy, and finds direct expression in the many characters who die by their own hand, literally cut with their own dust. At one level, suicide can be seen as one of the most useful dramatic conventions of the age; at another, it is nothing less than the definitive image of humanity's self-divided condition, and its tragic consequence that we are 'merely our own traitors'.

II

In discussing the place of suicide in Western thought prior to the Renaissance, a simple dichotomy between classical and Christian viewpoints is inadequate. There was no single view of suicide common to the different philosophical schools of antiquity, and many of the arguments used by Christian writers were derived from pagan philosophers. From a very early period, the starting point for any discussion of the ethics of suicide was a passage in Plato's *Phaedo*. While in the midst of claiming that the true philosopher should welcome death, Socrates adds the qualification that he should not kill himself, for 'they say it's forbidden'.[34] His primary argument derives from the idea that men are the possessions of the gods. To kill oneself is to claim rights over something which does not belong to one. This argument, together with the closely related belief, which he also mentions, that the soul has been placed in a prison, or perhaps garrison, from which it should not release itself until ordered, was to be extremely popular with Christian moralists. However, Socrates allows himself the escape-clause that God might in fact send such an order, and this possibility has been the source of endless controversy in both pagan and Christian moral philosophy. It is not altogether surprising that the *Phaedo* was later used to justify as well as condemn suicide: 'The Greek philosopher Cleombrotus is said to have been inspired by the *Phaedo* to drown himself, and Cato read the book through twice the night before he fell on his own sword.'[35] Similarly, although Plato, in the *Laws* (873*cd*), denies suicides the right to an honourable burial, he makes a list of exceptions—when the motive was compliance with state compulsion, the termination of incurable pain, or the avoidance of intolerable shame—which substantially qualifies any impression of criminality. As Donne commented, 'You see nothing is delivered by him [Plato] against it, but modestly, limitedly, and perplexedly.'[36]

Despite the survival of certain primitive customs (in Athens, the hand of the suicide was cut off and buried separately), the Greeks generally maintained a remarkably balanced attitude to the subject, avoiding the later excesses of Senecan enthusiasm on the one hand, and Christian outrage on the other. Thus Aristotle's condemnation of suicide is devoid of any trace of superstitious horror and is couched in terms of an injustice towards the community.[37] This argument, which is later also used by Aquinas, is the nearest approach by anyone to what many people today would consider the strongest and most obvious moral case against suicide: the hurtful effect on other people. The complete absence of this simple and powerful argument from all Renaissance and pre-Renaissance discussions of suicide is a striking instance of how truly alien from us past habits of thought often are.

The Greek dramatists seem to have recognised the value of suicide as a tragic act, as the deaths of Ajax, Antigone, Jocasta,

Phaedra, and Deianira testify, whilst avoiding any prejudgement of its morality. Greek Stoicism, as part of its general belief in the value of reason and the rightness of any decision made by a truly wise man, permitted suicide if the act was rationally motivated, but did not regard it as the ultimate freedom in the manner of Seneca.

> Far from being at the centre of Old Stoic ethical theory, suicide is, as it were, mentioned in passing. It is not being the arbiter of one's own life and death which makes the wise man the equal of the gods; it is his moral intention.[38]

The founder of the Stoic school, Zeno, who killed himself at the age of 72 after stumbling and breaking a toe, probably did so because he regarded his accident as the kind of divine summons mentioned by Plato, which a wise man should be ready to obey.

Greek writers on suicide, particularly Plato and Aristotle, were frequently quoted at the Renaissance, but Roman Stoicism and, more especially, the Stoicism of Seneca was just as great an influence. Seneca's highly individual version of Stoic philosophy might not unfairly be summed up by the formula 'All is for the best in the worst of all possible worlds'. In the monstrous atmosphere of Nero's Rome, the Stoic doctrine that no evil could befall the virtuous man was capable of only one interpretation: 'This is the one reason why we cannot complain of life: it keeps no one against his will.'[39] Whereas the Greek Stoics had regarded suicide tolerantly and dispassionately, Seneca venerated it as the one proof that the world could still be thought of as good, and man as free.

> The doctrine of suicide was indeed the culminating point of Roman Stoicism. The proud, self-reliant, unbending character of the philosopher could only be sustained when he felt that he had a sure refuge against the extreme forms of suffering or of despair.[40]

Seneca's own suicide, when he was out of favour with Nero, resolved the contradictions and hypocrisies of his position as both a moral philosopher and the agent of a murderous tyrant. (Amongst other things, he had been an accessory to the murder of

Agrippina and in fact composed Nero's explanation to the Senate.) By his death he also helped to vindicate his own rhetoric: 'For there is a very disgraceful charge often brought against our school—that we deal with the words, and not with the deeds, of philosophy.'[41] In fact, the many noble suicides in both Greek and Roman history were perhaps a more significant influence on Renaissance thought concerning this topic than the teachings of any school of philosophy about the 'rationality' of the act. The knowledge that so many of the best and bravest of the ancients had died by their own hand inevitably spurred a reconsideration of the ethics of suicide and even, if John Sym is to be believed, led to the occurrence of actual suicides:

> *The eighth* and last generall *motive*, whereupon *self-murderers* doe kill themselves, is frequent *examples* both of *heathens* and *Christians*, who have done the same, and are celebrated, and famous in *histories*, of whom we neither see, nor hear of further evil befallen them.[42]

I have suggested that Senecan enthusiasm for suicide was, in part, a response to the peculiar conditions of contemporary Roman society. Similarly, the extravagant praise of both Cato and Lucrece in classical literature was inextricably bound up with the political significance of their suicides. In all ages, society's attitude to suicide has been the product of various factors which have had little to do with any objective assessment of its morality. It remains to be determined what underlay the Christian opposition to suicide which first manifested itself in the third century AD, and grew gradually more vehement thereafter.

The Bible itself provides little basis for such an opposition, since the legitimacy of the act is nowhere discussed, and the various biblical suicides are recorded without any moralistic comment. Nor is there any direct connection with the pacifism and dislike of bloodshed that characterised the early Christians. By the time suicide began to be condemned by the Church, it had become common for Christians to enlist in the army, and in 314 the Council of Arles went so far as to excommunicate deserters. The basic explanation offered by Henry Fedden in his history of the topic is that Christian opposition to suicide had no origins in

Christian doctrine but was an upsurge of popular morality, a reversion to a primitive horror of suicide, that appeared when the Roman Empire began to break up: 'As rationalism and education decline so the penalties against suicide increase; and vice versa.'[43] The Christian prohibition was the result of 'an instinctive movement of the people,... it was imposed on the church from below.'[44] It is a weakness of Fedden's generally excellent study (a weakness shared by Georgia Noon's more recent but heavily derivative survey[45]) that belief in the right to kill oneself is too easily equated with 'progress' and 'rationality'. It could be claimed instead that Stoic arguments in favour of this 'right', like the similar views of the Enlightenment or the rather different ones of twentieth-century existentialism, are premised on an unrealistic notion of the individual's autonomy, and fail to acknowledge that all moral decisions have to be seen as part of a whole web of social and emotional relationships. Nevertheless, there is a genuine problem in explaining the strong reaction against suicide that developed in Christian teaching, and one of Fedden's other arguments seems particularly relevant. He points out that 'when any type of sacrificial suicide loses its social sanction, it becomes invested with a suicide horror which tends to be strong in direct ratio to the strength of the earlier sanction.'[46] The growth of ecclesiastical opposition to suicide coincided with a marked waning of enthusiasm for the idea of martyrdom. The blood of the martyrs may have been the seed of the Church, but the many thousands of deaths were the source of a sublimated guilt and horror which became transferred to the act of suicide. As Christianity moved from being a minority sect to a state religion, the other-worldly orientation which had produced so many eager martyrs needed to be tempered by the realities of social existence.

Nevertheless, it was not until St Augustine condemned it in *The City of God*, that suicide was inevitably destined to be regarded as a mortal sin: 'It is perhaps only the weight and influence of St Augustine that settles the question.'[47] His discussion of suicide (Book I, xv–xxvi) was provoked by a consideration of the many women who killed themselves rather than suffer rape when Alaric's forces captured Rome in 410AD. Such cases have always been a problem for Christian commentators and will be discussed fully in Chapter 5. The three most important general arguments employed by Augustine were that the sixth commandment referred to suicide as well as murder: '*Thou shalt not kill*, namely, *Neither thy self, or another. For he that kils him-selfe, kils no other but a man*';[48] that true greatness of spirit consisted in the endurance rather than the avoidance of calamity; and that one should not try to avoid one sin by committing another, since otherwise the obvious escape from inevitable contamination would be to kill oneself immediately after baptism. The last point shows again how Christianity was striving to bring its absolute and other-worldly idealism into a realistic ethical relation with normal life. What is interesting to note is that, although Augustine refers to the damnable despair of Judas, the association with despair is not yet a major consideration, and in fact represents a later rationalisation by the Church of a position which had been adopted as a consequence of other factors. Eight hundred years later, when Aquinas considered the topic, the association with despair was still relatively unimportant, his main arguments being that suicide was a sin against natural law, charity, the community, and God, from whom we had received life as a gift.[49]

In the years following St Augustine, there was a gradual increase in both ecclesiastical and legal sanctions against suicide, beginning with the Council of Braga (563), which forbade funeral rites and masses for suicides. This was the first Council to mention penalties for *all* suicides. Thirty years before, the Council of Orleans had forbidden funeral rites for those who killed themselves while accused of a crime.[50] In English law, this punitive trend reached its culmination during the mid-fourteenth century when suicides, except in cases of insanity, were declared to be *felo de se* and automatically liable to the confiscation of their property. The common practice of burying the suicide at a crossroads with a stake through his heart also originated during the Middle Ages. Though it never had a firm basis in law, it continued until the nineteenth century, the last recorded instance of burial at a crossroads being in 1823. Running parallel of course to this growing horror of suicide, and in strange contrast to it, was the literary sanctification, in accordance with the new courtly ideals, of those who died for love. Of the nine women whom Chaucer honours in his *Legend of Good Women*, five had killed themselves.

As far as actual suicides are concerned, within the main body of medieval society there appear to have been very few, though the absence of reliable records makes it impossible to be certain of this.[51] Outside that society, as heretic, witch, or Jew, there was the isolation which leads to despair and death. There were several cases of mass suicide among European Jews during the Middle Ages, and in France, the Albigensian heresy led to suicidal martyrdoms reminiscent of the early Christian period. The upheaval of the Reformation almost certainly produced an increase in suicide, as all such major social dislocations tend to do. More particularly, Protestant theology, by removing the saving power of the Church and its sacraments, insisting on the depravity of the human race, and encouraging constant self-scrutiny for signs of election or reprobation, undoubtedly increased the general level of spiritual anxiety. The most distinctive feature of Puritan casuistry became its efforts to combat the despair generated by its own theology. In one of the most thorough considerations of actual suicides in post-Reformation England, Michael MacDonald has suggested that historians, despite their common acceptance that a rise occurred during the sixteenth century, have seriously underestimated the level of suicide in Tudor and Stuart society.[52]

Most of the individual cases examined by MacDonald, being poor and illiterate, are unlikely to have been at all affected by any changed views of suicide which emerged from renewed interest in the classical past. Occasionally, however, the effect of this new frame of reference can be detected in the last words of actual as well as literary suicides. In 1537, Filippo Strozzi, a Florentine republican who was implicated in the assassination of Alessandro de' Medici, killed himself in prison, leaving behind a suicide note

> in which among other things, he commended his soul to God, with the prayer that, if no higher boon could be granted, he might at least be permitted to have his place with Cato of Utica and the other great suicides of antiquity.[53]

The impact of classical thought upon Renaissance attitudes to suicide was not simply a matter of increased familiarity with those philosophers who actually approved of suicide. There was a more general absorption of ideas about personal honour from a whole range of authors: 'Sir Thomas Elyot speaks for the common humanist attitude of the Renaissance, derived from Aristotle and Cicero as well as the Stoics, when he says, "all way dethe is to be preferred before servitude".'[54] Montaigne's partial defence of suicide in 'A Custome of the Île of Cea', and his frequent approving references elsewhere in the *Essayes*, stem from a deep knowledge and love of classical authors, particularly Seneca and Plutarch. His habit of contradicting himself (clearly discernible in the essay on suicide) arises from the difficulty of assimilating this revived classicism to Christian thought. Thus for Montaigne, 'The voluntariest death is the fairest', but he goes on to imply that suicide is cowardly by giving a Christianised rendering of the Stoic ideal of endurance: 'There is more constancie in using the chaine that holds us than in breaking the same; and more triall of stedfastnesse in Regulus than in Cato.'[55]

To some readers, Donne's *Biathanatos* has also appeared to be a work of self-contradiction, and it has been argued that its apparent contradictions are part of a deliberate attempt to fashion a sustained and witty formal paradox, a self-destroying argument about self-destruction. When the book *has* been credited with a coherent philosophical view of suicide, this has usually been claimed to be a sceptical and relativistic one and, indeed, the systematic way in which Donne undermines every traditional argument against suicide (whether regarded as an act against nature, reason, or God) does give an impression of moral relativism. Yet two recent co-editors of *Biathanatos*, in much the best account so far of the book's argument, show convincingly that Donne makes out a coherent and consistent case against any absolute prohibition on suicide, not by resorting to pure relativism but, on the contrary, by utilising traditional principles of Christian casuistry.[56] In applying moral theology to difficult individual cases, both Catholic and Protestant casuists had always been guided by the idea that the moral properties of any act are rooted in its motivation rather than its outward form. It is Donne's adoption of this kind of intentionalism which underpins superficially relativistic statements like the following: 'to me there appears no other interpretation safe but this, that there is no external act naturally evil, and that circumstances condition them, and give them their nature.'[57]

If all acts are to be judged by their intention then because, for

Christians, the highest of all moral intentions is to glorify God, there may be occasions when suicide is permissible on that basis: 'we say... that this may be done only when the honor of God may be promoved by that way and no other.'[58] Just as the normal commandment against killing another person may be superseded by a higher imperative, so may the commandment against self-killing. It is an important aspect of Donne's thoroughgoing intentionalist position that there is no real moral difference between acts of omission and acts of commission, between allowing oneself to be killed and actually killing oneself. It all depends on the motivation. Some martyrdoms may have been undertaken for selfish reasons, some suicides for holy ones. Furthermore, the logic of his approach leads inevitably to one final 'paradox'—that in some circumstances suicide may be morally *required*, may be a necessary part of moral perfection. Whether or not Christ actually shortened his time on the cross by a deliberate emission of his soul (and Donne believed that he did), there is little doubt that, for Donne, Christ was the great example of a 'pure' suicide, a self-chosen death entirely for the glory of God. The exact degree of agency shown by Jesus in bringing about his own death is not crucial to Donne's intentionalist argument: 'Not only does the law of God as set forth in Scripture not always prohibit suicide, but it reveals the very incarnation of God to be in fact a suicide Himself.'[59] Despite the apparent radicalism of this conclusion, nothing that Donne says suggests that the great majority of suicides are not in fact sinful in Christian terms. Few people would ever be able to achieve the purity of motive shown by Christ, and none of the usual justifications of suicide in classical philosophy (avoidance of pain or shame, a wise man's 'rational' choice) would be acceptable in the context of Donne's argument. Indeed, not the least remarkable aspect of *Biathanatos* is the way it avoids making any use of classical arguments in favour of suicide. Its interrogation of an established dogma is entirely by means of the premises and methods of Christian moral philosophy. The book is an excellent example of how the new familiarity with different philosophies and value-systems brought about not a simple substitution of classical ideas for Christian ones, but a general intellectual upheaval which took many forms.

The precise place of *Biathanatos* in any history of ideas is difficult to determine, partly because of the circumstances of its delayed publication, and partly because of its unusually personal significance. In the Preface, Donne admits that his own 'sickly inclination' to suicide was a major reason for writing the book:

> whensoever any affliction assails me, methinks I have the keys of my prison in mine own hand, and no remedy presents itself so soon to my heart as mine own sword.
> Often meditation of this hath won me to a charitable interpretation of their action who die so, and provoked me a little to watch and exagitate their reasons which pronounce so peremptory judgments upon them.[60]

A personal note may also be detected in some of Donne's arguments, such as his assertion that human beings do not always naturally desire to preserve themselves as Aquinas said, but have, on the contrary, a natural desire of dying. The relation of *Biathanatos* to its author's personal psychology is interestingly examined in Chapter 7 of John Carey's book on Donne.[61] Yet there are several indications that Donne, writing in the first decade of the seventeenth century, was treating 'a subject of emerging public, not perversely personal interest.'[62] In 1608, William Vaughan added fifteen chapters on suicide to the second edition of *The Golden Grove*; and four years later, Thomas Beard added a chapter on suicide to the second edition of *The Theatre of Gods Judgements*. It is also worthy of note that the English translations of Montaigne and Charron date from this period. In some sense, then, *Biathanatos* was a 'tract for the times',[63] and though not a direct influence on the drama, in the way that Montaigne's *Essayes* undoubtedly were, it shared something of the drama's characteristic mood during the 'Great Decade'. Both Donne and the dramatists show a strong sense of the complexities of any individual case and the difficulties of assimilating it to a general rule or dogma, yet also a determination not to abandon moral inquiry.

However, although Donne's intensive probing of behaviour and motive can be paralleled elsewhere in the period, as a writer on suicide he was ahead of his time. Even those moralists, influenced by pagan ethics, who show approval for the idea that death may be preferable to dishonour, manage to avoid, through their form of expression, any direct endorsement of suicide.[64] The increased discussion of the topic at the beginning of the seventeenth century consisted largely of a vigorous restatement of the old prohibitions. William Vaughan, mentioned above, is fairly typical in his emphatic denunciation of the act: 'Nothing is more damnable, nothing more ungodly, then for a man to slay himselfe.'[65] George Strode, in *The Anatomie of Mortalitie* (1618), gives a more eloquent rendering of the same viewpoint:

> for one to rend his owne body and soule in sunder (which God hath coupled together, and no man but hee must separate) is a sinne most horrible and fearefull, and breakes the bonds of God and Nature, and this no Beast (be it never so savage and cruell) will do.[66]

Interestingly enough, preachers did not shrink from attributing a cowardly desperation to the famous suicides of antiquity, so often praised by Renaissance writers: 'Brutus was held brave, but he despaired; Cato was said to be magnanimous, but he despaired; Antony was warlike, but driven by fear, he despaired.'[67] As this last quotation indicates, the extreme tone of Elizabethan and Jacobean writings against suicide was primarily the product of a belief that suicide necessarily involved a despair of salvation. The connection of suicide with despair, as important artistically as theologically, is what I now wish to consider.

III

In 1603, while imprisoned in the Tower, Sir Walter Ralegh tried to kill himself. Before making his unsuccessful attempt (the knife bounced off a rib), he wrote a farewell letter to his wife, part of which reads,

> Be not dismaide that I dyed in dispaire of gods mercies, strive not to dispute it but assure thy selfe that god hath not lefte me nor Sathan tempted me. Hope and dispaire live not together. I knowe it is forbidden to destroy our selfes but I trust it is forbidden in this sorte, that we destroye not ourselves dispairinge of gods mercie.[68]

For Ralegh, suicide was 'a disputable question, for divers doe hold opinion that a man may doe it and yett not desperatly dispayre of Gods Mercy but dy in Gods favour.'[69] Ralegh's exact state of mind when he wrote the letter can, of course, only be speculated upon. It may have been as complex and self-contradictory as that of any tragic protagonist.

> Ralegh's suicide note is the work of a man who seems to conceive of his identity as a dramatic role. . . . In the suicide attempt, he acted out his crushing self-pity and loneliness, his dark, fearful vision of oblivion, and perhaps a genuine longing for death. Paradoxically, he may also have intended his act to express heroic self-affirmation, the unwillingness of a Brutus 'to be made a wonder and a spectacle' for his enemies.[70]

In any event, the note, which is now thought to be authentic,[71] is a vivid contemporary illustration of the growing feeling, evident in Donne and Montaigne and exploited in poetry and drama, that suicide did not automatically signify religious despair. Before suicide could be regarded as in any way legitimate it was necessary to break its traditional association with despair, and for both Donne and Montaigne a consideration of historical suicides was sufficient to accomplish this. After quoting the story of Cleombrotus, Montaigne comments,

> Whereby it appeareth how improperly we call this voluntarie dissolution despaire; unto which the violence of hope doth often transport us, and as often a peacefull and setled inclination of judgement.[72]

Similarly, Donne's many examples culled from the 'Scriptures and other Histories', showed 'that none may justly say that all which kill themselves have done it out of a despair of God's mercy, (which is the only sinful despair)'.[73] Yet within the Christian tradition, the many noble suicides were overshadowed by the story of Judas, whose decision to hang himself after the betrayal of Christ became the standard example of sinful despair:

> by hanging of himselfe, he did rather augment then expiate the guilt of his wicked treacherie, because his despair of Gods mercy

in his damnable repentance, left no place in his soul for saving
repentance.[74]

As this quotation from St Augustine implies, despair was linked
with the inability to achieve a proper repentance, and it became a
firm belief that 'no sin at all but impenitency, can give testimony
of final reprobation.'[75] By its very nature, suicide was the one sin,
if considered as a sin, which left no room for repentance and this
partly explains the horror in which it came to be held, and the
gradual growth of its association with despair.

This association was fostered by numerous collections of
supposedly true stories of men who had become convinced of
their own damnation and killed themselves. One of the states of
mind which the Church Fathers had diagnosed as leading to
despair was Accidia—a sluggishness and paralysis of the will to
which monks were considered especially prone; hence it was that
many of these stories dealt with the suicides of monks or nuns.[76]
This genre flourished particularly after the Reformation, and the
most famous example, which appeared in many treatises on
despair, was that of Francis Spira, a Paduan lawyer who had
embraced the Protestant faith but had relapsed into Catholicism
under ecclesiastical pressure. His apostasy led to despair, and
despite many efforts to comfort him he eventually hanged
himself. His story was later dramatised by Nathaniel Woodes in
The Conflict of Conscience (printed 1591). Lily B. Campbell, in an
important article which established despair as Faustus's major sin
and the vital thread of Marlowe's play, placed *Doctor Faustus* in
direct line with such Puritan cases of conscience. As Campbell
wrote, in reference to the moment when Mephostophilis hands
Faustus a dagger (xviii. 57), 'The attempt at suicide is so much a
part of the sin of despair that it would be strange indeed if
Faustus's despair had not reached its climax in the traditional
manifestation.'[77] The symbolic use of the death of Judas, perhaps
the single most important source of this 'traditional
manifestation', is one instance of the way in which Christianity,
like other religions, continually seeks to embody its doctrines in
memorable images. Thus it was the role of suicide in the
iconography of despair, as much as any theological consideration,
which led to their close connection in the medieval and
Renaissance mind.

In one of the earliest and most influential of all allegorical poems, Prudentius's *Psychomachia*, it is the vice *Ira* who is depicted as stabbing herself, but by the thirteenth century it had become usual to represent a personified Despair in this posture. Medieval paintings frequently showed despairing figures hanging, drowning, or stabbing themselves,[78] and, given that such an association is not prominent in medieval theology, 'the insistence on suicide as a result of despair that we find in literature may owe much to the visual arts.'[79] Renaissance poets multiplied the forms of death which characterised despair, and took an apparent delight in cataloguing them. In Sylvester's translation of Du Bartas's *The Divine Weeks and Works* (1605), 'mad *Dispaire*' bears with her,

> burning Coales and Cordes,
> Aspes, Poysons, Pistols, Haltars, Knives, and swords.[80]

Marlowe's Faustus gives a similar list when he describes the despair into which he has fallen since the pact with Mephostophilis:

> My heart is harden'd, I cannot repent.
> Scarce can I name salvation, faith, or heaven,
> But fearful echoes thunders in mine ears,
> 'Faustus, thou art damn'd;' Then guns and knives,
> Swords, poison, halters, and envenom'd steel
> Are laid before me to dispatch myself.
>
> (vi. 18–23)

However, it was the rope and dagger (the main props of Spenser's 'man of hell, that cals himself *Despaire*') which were chiefly used to emblematise despair in the drama. They appear frequently in the Morality plays, either carried by Despair himself or some other agent of the devil,[81] and they continue to be used symbolically in the later secular drama. Hieronimo in *The Spanish Tragedy*, before delivering a despairing soliloquy, enters '*with a poniard in one hand, and a rope in the other*' (III.xii); and in Marston's *Antonio's Revenge*, Strotzo attempts to act out the role of a man stricken with despairing remorse and appears with '*a cord about his neck*' (IV.i. 156). Even in a late play such as

Massinger's *Believe as you List* (licensed 1631), this convention
appears in unaltered and medieval form when the imprisoned
Antiochus is presented with 'a poniard & halter' by his gaoler
(IV.ii).

The despair which the rope and dagger came to symbolise was a
specifically religious despair,

> an evill through which a man. . . is past all hope of the good will of
> God, verily thinking that his naughtinesse, or sinnes, excell the
> mercies and goodness of God; according to that saying of the first
> desperat man *Cain*; *Mine iniquitie is greater then can be pardoned.*[82]

Despair in this narrow sense remains important in the Jacobean
drama (more important, perhaps, than is generally recognised),
but in many of the plays it is transmuted to a more generalised
sense of hopelessness, something closer to the modern idea of
despair. This change finds a parallel outside the drama in *The
Anatomy of Melancholy*, where Burton continually oscillates
between a specific and a general use of the word. Thus he begins
his description of religious despair with a surprisingly broad
definition (ultimately derived from Cicero) which, one feels,
could be applied to the despair of Shakespeare's tragic heroes, as
well as to that of Faustus: 'a sickness of the soul without any hope
or expectation of amendment: which commonly succeeds fear;
for whilst evil is expected, we fear: but when it is certain, we
despair.'[83] Undoubtedly the tendency, shared by Burton, of
writers in this period to refer to all suicides as 'despairing'
whatever their motives may have been contributed to a widening
of the meaning of despair. Thus Sir William Denny in his poem
on suicide, *Pelecanicidium* (1653), makes a survey of the various
suicidal 'types', who include 'Lovers', 'Great Spirits', 'The
unfortunate Merchant', 'The curious Zealot', and 'The Bloody
Murtherer'. Although obviously rather different cases, they are
collectively addressed as 'Desperate Souls'.

More importantly, such a widening of meaning can be seen as
part of the fundamental changes that were taking place in society,
as part of the gradual progress towards the secular. In the drama
this progress entailed, among other things, changes in the
presentation and language of despair. Hamlet does not clutch a
rope and dagger as he thinks of suicide; the promptings to self-

murder come from within him, not from an evil angel or a personified Despair; the language of his soliloquies is free from the conventional phrases associated with religious despair. These changes, though, must be seen in the context of a surprising continuity of thought and image. Claudius's speech in the prayer scene, for instance, contains such traditional elements as a reference to Cain (along with Judas the archetype of religious despair), and an attempt to 'look up' to heaven for mercy. Changes in presentation and emphasis do not necessarily imply changes in fundamental meaning. Just as the many heroic suicides in the drama were 'not read at the time as a direct humanist thesis in the ethics of suicide,'[84] so the different dramatic uses of suicide's connection with despair (in both its narrower and broader senses) represent, not an assault on Christian orthodoxy, but an exploitation of the Christian tradition for the purposes of tragedy.

IV

The way in which individual dramatists incorporated the different implications of suicide into their plays tells us much about their art, less about their ethical viewpoint. Of the better-known playwrights, only Massinger and Chapman have a clearly detectable 'ethical bias', the former towards an orthodox Christian horror of suicide, the latter towards a neo-Stoic approval of it. In general, dramatic treatments of suicide are governed by a pragmatic awareness of its capacity to symbolise nobility as well as guilt and despair. Heywood, a highly prolific man of the theatre with no claims to being, in Shaw's phrase, an 'artist-philosopher', makes use of both faces of suicide with equal facility in his series of dramatisations of classical mythology. Deianira's suicide in *The Brazen Age* (1610–13) is an honourable atonement for her fatal gift to Hercules:

> when she heard the tortures of her Lord,
> And what effect her fatall present tooke,
> Exclaim'd on *Nessus*, and to prove herself
> Guiltlesse of treason in her husbands death,
> With her own hand she boldly slue herselfe.

Tellamon: That noble act proclaim'd her innocent,
        And cleares all blacke suspition.
                                (V. vol. III, p.255)[85]

This is true to the spirit as well as the form of the Greek story, but
in the second part of *The Iron Age* (1612–13) Heywood makes use
of traditions that Helen of Troy killed herself to achieve a totally
different effect. After surveying her 'wrinkled forehead' in a
looking-glass, and wondering how it launched a thousand ships,
she gives a short speech on the transitory nature of beauty before
committing suicide. As well as exemplifying the medieval theme
of *vanitas*, her death illustrates the reward that follows sin. She
calls it 'The guerdon of Adultery, Lust, and Pride' and Ulysses,
acting as Epilogue, says 'In thee they are punisht' (V. vol. III,
p. 430). Heywood simply moves from one frame of reference
to another in order to achieve the appropriate dramatic
image.

In many plays, the desired response can only be elicited by a
'metaphysical' union of opposites. When Orgilus bleeds himself
to death at the end of Ford's *The Broken Heart*, the onlookers'
comments are 'Desperate courage' and 'Honourable infamy'
(V.ii. 123). Similarly, when Cato kills himself in the anonymous
university play *Caesar's Revenge* (c.1592–96), his son, who has
an earlier speech condemning suicide as an act of cowardice,
declares,

> I know not whether I should more lament,
> That by thine owne hand thou thus slaughtred art,
> Or Joy that thou so nobly didst depart.
>   (ll.1141–3)

Such ambivalence was capable of more than one form of dramatic
development. The two most successful playwrights of the age,
Shakespeare and Fletcher, both show great awareness of the
varied connotations of suicide, but differ considerably in their use
of them. As Una Ellis-Fermor wrote, the 'Beaumont and
Fletcher' plays

> do not raise, by the implications of the material they choose and
> the passions they stir, those issues touching the meaning of life

and the destiny of man which run through... [earlier Jacobean] tragedies. But alongside this there is a marked increase in explicit statement and in discussion, if not of the main tragic issues, of topics of still living and immediate concern.[86]

A good example of this 'explicit statement' and 'discussion' is the long argument in *Bonduca* (1611–14) between Penyus and Petillius as to whether the former should kill himself. The way in which Fletcher illuminates differing notions of repentance and honour by staging this debate is dealt with fully in Chapter 4. The whole argument has a certain academic remoteness which is particularly apparent in the secondary discussion which develops concerning which *method* of suicide would be most appropriate. Penyus at first proposes to hang himself, 'a most base death, /Fitting the basenesse of my fault', or perhaps to poison himself. Petillius, who wishes him to die honourably, will not let him do either but makes him agree to fall on his sword:

> your sword must do the deed:
> 'Tis shame to die choak'd, fame to die and bleed.
> (IV.iii. 146–7)

With remarkable intuition, Fletcher has grasped the definite, though normally subconscious connection between different means of suicide and the different responses to it. For various reasons, some of them very deep-rooted, hanging has always been the form of suicide to inspire the greatest horror. Amidst the general Roman toleration of suicide, there was a remarkable survival of older superstitions in a law forbidding burial to those who had hanged themselves. In the Christian era, hanging was directly equated with despair through the story of Judas, and the consideration (implied in Fletcher's use of the word 'choak'd') that this form of death left one unable to call for mercy and achieve a last-minute repentance.[87] In the drama, suicides for honour *never* hang themselves; almost invariably they 'die and bleed', thus imitating the many Roman heroes who fell on their own swords, as well as hinting at both religious and medical doctrines concerning the beneficial effects of bloodshed. All these implications are contained in the lines quoted above, which are a marvellous compression of the Renaissance ambivalence towards

suicide. Although Fletcher's acute perception of this ambivalence
is integrated with the play's general investigation of honour and
dishonour, especially in relation to male and female roles (suicide
can be either 'manly' or 'the death of rats, and women'), one feels
that the debate which springs up over the implications of
Penyus's death is more important to Fletcher than the death
itself. The complexity is abstract and intellectual rather than
emotional and fully dramatic.

In Fletcher and Massinger's *Thierry and Theodoret*, there is a
similarly acute expression of the equivocal Christian attitude to
voluntary death. The veiled Ordella is told that she must die for
Thierry's sake, and in some very fine lines she nobly brushes aside
the fear of death:

> Thierry: 'Tis terrible.
> Ordella: 'Tis so much the more noble.
> Thierry: 'Tis full of fearefull shaddowes.
> Ordella: So is sleepe Sir,
>   Or any thing that's meerely ours and mortall,
>   We were begotten gods else; but those feares
>   Feeling but once the fires of nobler thoughts,
>   Fly, like the shapes of clouds we forme, to nothing.
>   (IV.i. 89–94)

Thierry and his friend Martell regard this readiness to die as a
form of martyrdom ('Thou shalt be sainted woman...'), but
when Ordella's identity is revealed the whole scene inverts itself.
Thierry can no longer kill Ordella, but she still wishes to die for
him. When she '*Drawes a knife*', Martell gives a lengthy
denunciation of suicide which neatly balances the previous praise
for her willingness to be sacrificed:

>   where, or how
>   Got you these bloody thoughts? what divell durst
>   Looke on that Angell face, and tempt? do you know
>   What 'tis to die thus, how you strike the stars,
>   And all good things above? do you feele
>   What followes a selfe blood, whither you venter,
>   And to what punishment?
>   (IV.i. 208–14)

Undoubtedly it was the opportunity of juxtaposing the sacrificial and suicidal aspects of martyrdom which determined the form of this scene, one of the finest in the Beaumont and Fletcher canon, and became its *raison d'être*. As E.M. Waith said of the Beaumont and Fletcher plays in general: 'The shape of the conflict which is essential to all dramatic action is preserved, proliferating in endless oppositions, even though the conflict signifies nothing beyond itself.'[88] In Shakespeare, the conflict which is inherent in Renaissance attitudes to suicide is not localised in carefully staged debates nor treated purely abstractly, but is both an integral part of the play's overall design and a crucial aspect of the hero's anguished self-division. This can best be seen by an examination of *Hamlet*.

In *Hamlet*, the problem of suicide is a part of the general problem of action that faces the protagonist. Shakespeare inherited a dramatic tradition, evident in *The Spanish Tragedy* and *Antonio's Revenge*, that one of the obstacles facing the revenger was his own despair and possible suicide. This convention is employed by Shakespeare to link suicide and revenge as two parallel elements in a general articulation of the moral ambiguity of all human action or, for that matter, inaction. Made painfully aware of the evil which inheres in life, first by his mother's move from a 'celestial bed' to 'prey on garbage' and then by the revelation of his father's 'most horrible' murder, Hamlet, like any other person, has two main courses open to him—either he can withdraw from life and its corruption, ultimately by suicide, or he can act to remedy that corruption. Initially, of course, there is no action which suggests itself as a remedy and, in the first soliloquy, the emotional drive is towards abdication from life. The Ghost's tale of murder, by invoking all the natural loyalties of son to father, initiates an equally powerful emotional drive towards remedial action, the 'wild justice' of revenge.

In one sense, then, the impulses towards suicide and revenge are directly opposed means of confronting the situation, but thematically they are developed as parallels. For in each case, the strong and natural emotional pull is countered by an awareness of the moral dangers attending the proposed action. The death-longing of the first soliloquy finds its check in the reflection that the Everlasting *has* 'fixed /His canon 'gainst self-slaughter'

(I.ii. 131-2). A similarly orthodox moral sense restrains the headlong rush to revenge by producing the thought that

> The spirit that I have seen
> May be a devil, and the devil hath power
> T'assume a pleasing shape, yea, and perhaps
> Out of my weakness and my melancholy,
> As he is very potent with such spirits,
> Abuses me to damn me.
>
> (II.ii. 584-9)

It is interesting to note that in the poem which I began this book by quoting from, Copley's *A Fig for Fortune*, suicide and revenge are linked together as successive temptations of the melancholy man, temptations which are diabolically inspired. The frequently devilish nature of the desire for revenge has been amply documented by Eleanor Prosser in *Hamlet and Revenge*, but of course, as is explained so well by Harold Jenkins in his long-awaited Arden edition of the play, what is most important about revenge and most dramatically useful to Shakespeare is its moral ambiguity. Filial duty and the need to reform a rotten state are balanced by the imperatives against murder and regicide. This ambiguity is insisted on in many different ways throughout the play, but is seen most clearly and simply in Hamlet's belief that he is prompted to his revenge by heaven *and* hell (II.ii. 570). Also important is the way the action is organised so that the protagonist becomes both the agent and the victim of revenge.

> The situation of revenge is revealed as one in which the same man may act both parts; and the paradox of man's dual nature, compound of nobility and baseness, god and beast, repeatedly placed before us in the words of the play and represented in its action in the contrasting brother kings, is also exemplified in the hero's dual role.[89]

The morally paradoxical self-identity of agent and victim is something which is also central to the idea of suicide, but the ambiguity which is more precisely Shakespeare's concern is the way suicide can be considered either as a form of resolute action or as a sin against conscience. It is this uncertainty which permits it to be linked with revenge in the 'To be or not to be' soliloquy as twin examples in a highly ambivalent argument about what is the 'nobler' thing to do when confronted by life's miseries.

The dominant question of the soliloquy—whether life is preferable to death—is clearly more directly related to suicide than to revenge, yet a linkage is effected almost immediately when Hamlet poses the subsidiary question concerning how life, if chosen in preference to death, should be lived. Is it nobler to endure passively the blows of fortune or to combat them actively? The obvious hopelessness of taking arms against a 'sea' of troubles suggests that defeat and death will follow automatically; that one might just as well have chosen the bare bodkin in the first place rather than the avenger's sword. It is the hopeless, 'suicidal' appearance of all forms of action which produces the apparently disjunctive exclamation, 'To die...', and a reconsideration of death as the better alternative. The bulk of the soliloquy then shows why the superficially attractive option of death is not taken. We are held back from suicide by a dread of what the after-life might be like, and it is this fear 'that makes us rather bear those ills we have /Than fly to others that we know not of' (III.i. 81–2). Revenge has slipped out of Hamlet's consideration for most of the soliloquy, but is brought into a relation with suicide again by the lines which immediately follow, the famous and often misinterpreted

> Thus conscience does make cowards of us all,
> And thus the native hue of resolution
> Is sicklied o'er with the pale cast of thought,
> And enterprises of great pitch and moment
> With this regard their currents turn awry
> And lose the name of action.
>   (III.i. 83–8)

The first thing to establish is that, despite all those critics who have chosen to adopt the rarer meaning 'consciousness' (turning the play into a 'Tragedy of Thought'), there is no good reason to take 'conscience' other than in its normal sense of 'moral conscience', the capacity to distinguish between right and wrong. All seven other uses of the word in the play point to this sense, and only a few lines earlier the usual meaning has been given highly dramatic emphasis as part of our first definite evidence of Claudius's guilt ('How smart a lash that speech doth give my conscience!' (III.i. 50)). The reading 'moral conscience' has been convincingly argued for by Catherine Belsey,[90] who goes on to point out that the superficially negative association with cowardice can be found elsewhere in Shakespeare in contexts which make it clear that we should approve rather than disapprove of this kind of 'cowardice'. Richard III, on the eve of Bosworth, is afflicted by 'coward conscience' for the first time in the play (V.iii. 180), before dismissing it in unmistakably Machiavellian terms:

> Conscience is but a word that cowards use,
> Devised at first to keep the strong in awe.
>   (V.iii. 310–11)

His rejection of conscience is prefigured by the Second Murderer of Clarence, who is able to carry out his orders only by avoiding meddling with conscience, for 'it makes a man a coward' (I.iv. 131–2). The context in which Hamlet makes the association with cowardice is one of suicide rather than murder, but in orthodox Christian morality this of course makes no real difference. If it is fear which makes us hold back from suicide, then this sort of fear should be encouraged rather than dismissed. The most pertinent parallel to be found in Shakespeare's other works occurs in *Cymbeline*, where Imogen reflects

>   Against self-slaughter
> There is a prohibition so divine
> That cravens my weak hand.
>   (III.iv. 76–8)

Here there can be little doubt that the 'cowardice' shown is not to be condemned.

If Hamlet's self-rebuke cannot be taken at face-value when it alludes to suicide, how, then, is it to be taken when it seems to refer to revenge? What is the relation between 'Thus conscience does make cowards of us all' and the rest of the sentence following 'And thus', which appears to return to the question of revenge? In the notes to the Arden edition, Harold Jenkins argues that the relationship is primarily one of analogy.

> In fact there is no necessity to see ll.84–8 as concerned with
> 'conscience' at all. Resolution weakens in the course of thinking
> just as courage to face death weakens through the operation of
> conscience.[91]

I would dissent from this on several grounds, and would suggest
that the relation of suicide to other kinds of action (including
revenge) is much closer than this, and hence that the opposition
of 'conscience' to 'resolution' is much stronger than Jenkins
suggests. Hamlet, held back from suicide by considerations of
'coward conscience', is directly opposed to Laertes the 'resolute'
revenger who exclaims,

> Conscience and grace, to the profoundest pit!
> I dare damnation.
>
> $\qquad\qquad\qquad$ (IV.v. 132–3)

The merging of one moral problem with another is eased by the
fact that suicide (although often condemned as a cowardly
abdication from action) could also be thought of as an act of brave
'resolution', as in Cleopatra's promise, 'My resolution and my
hands I'll trust,/ None about Caesar' (IV.xv. 49–50). The
association with suicide suggests in itself that 'resolution' may not
always be the simple positive that it is often taken to be, and
Catherine Belsey lists a number of examples in Shakespeare where
the word and its cognates seem 'to convey the desperate courage
of a criminal rather than the determination of a hero.'[92] The most
important of these in the present context is the reference
to young Fortinbras as having 'Sharked up a list of lawless
resolutes' (I.i. 98) for the invasion of Denmark. This, together
with his later invasion of Poland which risks the death of 20,000
men for 'an eggshell', strongly suggests that a thoughtful holding
back from resolute enterprises may have a great deal to be said for
it. A second particularly significant Shakespearean use of
'resolute' occurs when one of Clarence's murderers rebukes the
other for holding back: 'I thought thou hadst been resolute' (I.iv.
112). As in *Hamlet*, there is a direct opposition to conscience
involved here. The significance of these examples can be

confirmed by noting the same antithesis in Fletcher, Massinger, and Field's *The Knight of Malta* (one villain tells another 'never think of conscience;/There is none to a man resolv'd' (II.iii.Cam.V, p.137)), and by observing the frequent collocation of resolution with despair in Renaissance literature. Marston's Antonio calls comfort 'a flatt'ring Jack' which 'melts resolved despair' (*Antonio's Revenge*, I.v. 49–50), and Marlowe's Faustus exclaims,

> What boots it then to think of God or heaven?
> Away with such vain fancies, and despair;
> Despair in God, and trust in Beelzebub.
> Now go not backward; no, Faustus, be resolute.
>   (v. 3–6)[93]

By bringing suicide—a form of 'resolute' action which springs from despair and which conscience checks—into a close relation with all other kinds of 'resolute' enterprise (including revenge), Shakespeare has managed to make all possible action a matter of moral doubt and uncertainty, confirming in a new way the ambiguities about revenge which have been present all along. In the face of this, the only answer consistently suggested by the great soliloquy is that we should passively endure life's evils, holding back from both suicide and vengeful action. Since such a passive acceptance is prompted by moral fear rather than moral confidence, it too may be considered ambiguous, perhaps as much cowardly as noble. As the play progresses, this middle way of acceptance comes to seem more definitely praiseworthy. This is because it attaches itself to a belief in Providence, 'a divinity that shapes our ends', and hence does not mean a complete withdrawal from action since Providence can be trusted to provide opportunities to act on behalf of justice in ways which are not morally tainted.

The emotionally compelling but morally suspect choices which Hamlet holds back from in the 'To be or not to be' soliloquy, are of course enacted for us in the play by the two children of Polonius. The sharp dramatic contrast between Laertes, the headstrong and treacherous revenger, and Hamlet, the reflective and reluctant one, is particularly important. The comparison with Ophelia is less schematic, yet the difference between

Ophelia's maimed funeral rites and Hamlet's military exit from the stage ('The soldiers' music and the rites of war/Speak loudly for him' (IV.ii. 388-9)) takes on a special significance when one remembers the traditional argument against suicide, often cited during the Renaissance, which likened the soul to a soldier on guard duty who cannot leave his post until ordered by his Commander.[94] The fact that Ophelia, as someone who was clearly insane at the time of her death, would in practice have been entitled to a full Christian burial, makes it all the more likely that a thematically significant contrast is intended here. Yet the 'doubtful' nature of Ophelia's death, the legalistic quibbling of the clowns, and Laertes' spirited denunciation of the 'churlish priest', all give a sense of continued moral inquiry rather than the straightforward fulfilment of a moral design. And of course we must remember that Ophelia and Laertes were driven to their extreme courses of action by Hamlet's inability to control such tendencies in himself, his moment of vengeful passion leading to the death of Polonius, and his strong desire to withdraw from life and the means by which life is continued leading to his rejection of Ophelia and her love.

It could be argued also that the accumulation of evidence which will permit morally unambiguous action results only in the accumulation of avoidable catastrophes. Yet the play as a whole seems to move towards an endorsement of Hamlet's middle course between extremes, his Stoic acceptance of life's ills which becomes coupled with a trust in Providence to provide the opportunity for noble action. The main dramatic function of Horatio, a man 'that is not passion's slave', 'A man that Fortune's buffets and rewards' has 'ta'en with equal thanks' (III.ii. 64-5), is to image this kind of Stoic ideal. It is one of the play's last ironies that Hamlet should have to prevent Horatio from killing himself, his Stoicism proving to be of the 'antique Roman' variety. We are dramatically reminded that in some philosophies noble endurance and suicide are *not* necessarily incompatible, thus reopening all the doubts and questions of the 'To be or not to be' soliloquy.

In his Introduction to the Arden edition, Harold Jenkins asks, 'Is it not indeed the ambivalence which Shakespeare perceives in revenge that invites into the play all those ideas about the dual nature of man, mingling good and evil, which ultimately give it shape?'[95] I hope I have shown how suicide, by also being an action in which conscience may oppose resolution, plays its full part in supporting such a dramatic design, operating in close conjunction with revenge to generate a complex and deeply-felt debate about what is the 'nobler' course to pursue. In *Hamlet*, the equivocal nature of suicide is exploited by Shakespeare in an altogether more fundamental way than in the plays of Fletcher and his collaborators.

As I wrote at the beginning of this chapter, it is the clash of opposing implications in a stage suicide which offers the most obvious dramatic potential. Yet when a playwright is attempting to use suicide to make a specific and limited point, the extra connotations can prove an embarrassment. This is the theme which runs through the following chapter, which looks at suicide and despair as the rewards of sin, and which may be fittingly prefaced by a quotation from *Biathanatos*: 'Death, therefore, is an act of God's justice, and when He is pleased to inflict it, He may choose His officer, and constitute myself as well as any other.'[96]

CHAPTER 2

Retribution

Thus doth He force the swords of wicked men
To turn their own points in their masters' bosoms.
(Shakespeare)

When Fulke Greville wrote that the purpose of modern tragedy
was 'to point out Gods revenging aspect upon every particular
sin, to the despaire, or confusion of mortality',[1] he was correctly
characterising the pattern of most Elizabethan and Jacobean
tragedy, though not the essence of its greatest achievements. This
idea that retribution for sin was the principal explanation for a fall
into adversity had gradually grown more prominent in the course
of the sixteenth century. Medieval tragedy had been surprisingly
little concerned with the relationship of sin to punishment. The
great symbol of tragedy for the Middle Ages was the Wheel of
Fortune. All who put their trust in earthly things were liable to be
rolled round to the bottom of the Wheel, whether they were
sinful or just. Indeed, the fall of a just man was a better example of
the random effects of Fortune. The original collections of verse
narratives of the falls of princes (the primary medieval tragic
form) made little use of the idea of poetic justice. This is how
Chaucer's Monk records the suicide of Nero:

> Him-self he slow, he coude no better reed,
> Of which fortune lough, and hadde a game.[2]

In Lydgate to some extent, and more particularly in the
sixteenth-century extensions to Lydgate—the various editions of
the *Mirror for Magistrates*—death and suffering begin to be more
closely related to the sins of the sufferer. Jack Cade, in the 1559
Mirror, wonders whether to blame Fortune or his own folly:

37

> What ever it were this one poynt sure I know,
> Which shall be mete for every man to marke:
> Our lust and wils our evils chefely warke.[3]

Interestingly enough, this growing connection of character with event occurs at the same time that the presentation of these tragical tales becomes more dramatic. Whereas Boccaccio and Lydgate had narrated most of their stories, the characters in the *Mirror* usually tell their own stories in the form of a 'complaint'.

Three other developments which influenced the retributive character of Jacobean tragedy were the tendency to moralise Seneca's influential portrayals of great crimes and bloody revenges (Seneca 'beateth down sinne', according to one of his Elizabethan translators);[4] the frequently ironic reversals of fortune in continental prose fiction which could be used as evidence of sin's tendency to destroy itself ('Marke how he himselfe made the Net wherein he was intangled, and whetteth the knyfe where on he myserably ended his lyfe');[5] and the tendency, noted in the last chapter, of the later Morality plays to concentrate on the damnation of the wicked man rather than the redemption of the average man.

All these developments were, properly speaking, perhaps symptoms rather than influences—symptoms of the prevailing theories of the ethical value of literature. Without exception, Elizabethan and Jacobean defenders of the drama describe their art in didactic terms. Thus for Chapman 'the soul, limbs, and limits of an autentical tragedy' were 'material instruction, elegant and sententious excitation to virtue, and deflection from her contrary.'[6] Heywood, in his *Apology for Actors* (1612), echoes this in more concrete terms:

> If we present a Tragedy, we include the fatall and abortive ends of such as commit notorious murders, which is aggravated and acted with all the Art that may be, to terrifie men from the like abhorred practises.[7]

Such statements have the air of being useful propaganda against the theatre's many attackers, rather than representing a deeply-considered analysis of extremely complex works of art, and indeed it is the major disappointment of Renaissance literary theory that it is unable to offer an adequate account of the best literature of its own period. After saying this, however, it remains true that the didactic concept of inevitable punishment for sin is the major shaping influence on the basic structure of most Renaissance tragedies. The many 'acts of death' that constitute the Elizabethan idea of tragedy are the 'gateway by which the sanctions of the next world enter mundane experience'.[8] Sometimes retribution is clearly and crudely of supernatural origin. Faustus and the Borgia Pope, Alexander VI, are both dragged by devils into a literal and visible hell; Malefort Senior in *The Unnatural Combat* and Antiochus in *Pericles* are struck down by a flash of lightning, a 'fire from heaven'; D'Amville miraculously knocks his own brains out in a deliberately incredible 'accident'. Yet Faustus suffers terribly in this world as well. His despair is not only a fear of punishment, but a punishment itself. In the secularisation of the theme of guilt and punishment that we find in the mature drama, the depiction of heaven's judgements in earthly terms, suicide and despair had a vital role to play. That role is the subject of this chapter.

One of the more subtle ideas in both Christian and classical teaching on guilt and retribution is that punishment does not *follow* sin but is born the same instant via the operation of the sinner's conscience.[9] A passage in Plutarch's *Moralia*, a favourite source of pagan wisdom during the Renaissance, makes this point eloquently:

> . . .mischievous wickednesse frameth of her selfe, the engines of her own torment, as being a wonderfull artisan of a miserable life, which (together with shame and reproch) hath in it lamentable calamities, many terrible frights, fearefull perturbations and passions of the spirit, remorse of conscience, desperate repentance, and continuall troubles and unquietnesse.[10]

This is the significance of the 'terrible dreams' that nightly shake the Macbeths and the fearful madness that overtakes Ferdinand and Sir Giles Overreach. Bosola calls Ferdinand's lycanthropia a 'fatal judgement', and in the section of Goulart's *Admirable and Memorable Histories* from which Webster derived the details of

Ferdinand's affliction, there is a comment which epitomises the manner in which such judgements are often made in the drama:

> GOD needes not to seeke far for any rods to scourge us, seeing that wee carry them in our own bowels.[11]

The evil man carries his own hell within him and can no more escape punishment than fly from himself. In a wider, more truly tragic sense, every man is his own traitor, 'every man... the greatest enemy unto himself'. Given the traditional association of the guilty conscience with suicide and the inevitable Elizabethan practice of 'concluding tragedy with death and giving it a final seal of authenticity in death',[12] one would tend naturally to conclude that a despairing suicide was the most artistically satisfactory way of terminating a life of sin. Indeed, suicide was often regarded as symbolising God's punishment of the sinner. Acknowledging this, Donne tried to use it as an argument against the sinfulness of the act: 'And if it be, as others affirm, *poena peccati*, it is then *involuntarium*, which will hardly consist with the nature of sin.'[13] The more popular view, exemplified by Thomas Beard and many others, was to have it both ways. Suicide was both crime and punishment:

> yea the verie act it selfe is both a crime and a judgement; a crime deserving a further judgement, even eternall damnation in hell fire; and a judgement and punishment of some notable sinnes committed by them before, and of an ungodlie and wicked life unrepented of.[14]

Arbaces has this idea in mind, at the end of Beaumont and Fletcher's *A King and No King*, when he tells the worried Mardonius that he has not committed enough other sins to think of killing himself yet. When he comes to it at last,

> Ile tell thee: then I shall be such a creature,
> That thou wilt give me leave without a word.
>
> (V.iv. 36–7)

Only the most wicked men kill themselves, and by the time they have sunk low enough to do so, their suicide acts as a judgement on their other crimes. As was mentioned in the previous chapter this pattern was present in many of the Morality plays and was naturally carried over into the early Elizabethan drama, via such hybrid historical Moralities as *Apius and Virginia*. Thus the ambitious and treacherous Humber drowns himself in despair in *Locrine* (1591–95) and, on the brink of the Jacobean period, we find the suicide of Will Brand in *The Death of Robert Earl of Huntingdon* (1598) being carefully made to symbolise despair and retribution. Brand has been King John's ruthless agent, his 'instrument of death', and has been implicitly contrasted with Hubert who remains loyal to the King while trying to mitigate his crimes. After Brand has forced Matilda to drink the poison sent by John, despair suddenly and unsubtly overwhelms this previously unfeeling monster. He

> now will hurry to damnations mouth,
> Forst by the gnawing worme of conscience.
> (ll.2625–6)

His death, as reported by a servant, is obviously a conscious conflation of the two versions of Judas Iscariot's death:[15]

> Borne with a violent rage, he clim'd a tree,
> And none of us could hinder his intent:
> But getting to the top boughes, fast he tied
> His garters to his necke, and a weake branch,
> Which being unable to sustaine his weight,
> Downe to the ground he fell, where bones and flesh
> Lie pasht together, in a poole of blood.
> (ll.2689–95)

The moralisation of this image of despair, the *sententia* which completes the emblem, follows immediately in the Earl of Oxford's comment:

> Alas for woe; but this is just heavens doome
> On those that live by bloode: in bloode they die.
> (ll.2696–7)

Contributing to the use of suicide as an image of retribution is the constant pressure of metaphor on action that we find in Jacobean plays. According to Hereward T. Price, Webster gives us a 'double construction, an outer and an inner... He gives us figure in action and figure in language. These he fuses so intimately as to make the play one entire figure.'[16] Thus, to take an immediately relevant example, Claudius in *Hamlet*, Bianca in *Women Beware Women*, and Hippolita in *'Tis Pity She's a Whore* vividly enact Macbeth's metaphor for 'even-handed justice' which

> Commends th'ingredience of our poisoned chalice
> To our own lips.
>
> (I.vii. 11–12)

The man who falls by his own hand is able to symbolise with peculiar aptness both the hand of God buffeting the sinner and the divided nature of the guilt-stricken conscience which 'for want of other evidences... produceth our selves against our selves.'[17] D'Amville's death in *The Atheist's Tragedy*, by accidentally knocking his own brains out with an axe, is heavy with overtones of suicide. The dialogue following the 'accident' neatly links crime with punishment, murder with self-murder:

D'Amville:	What murderer was he
	That lifted up my hand against my head?
1st Judge:	None but yourself, my Lord.
D'Amville:	I thought he was
	A murderer that did it.

> (V.ii. 243–6)

His death is in direct line of descent from that of Cambyses in Preston's play of that name printed about 1569. After a life of cruelty, his own sword slips out of its sheath and stabs him. Tourneur may also have had in mind Thomas Beard's account of Marlowe's death in a tavern brawl. According to Beard, Marlowe was grabbed by the wrist and caused to stab himself with his own dagger. This symbolic 'suicide' was the most fitting way God's judgement could descend on an atheist, Beard tells us:

But herein did the justice of God most notably appeare, in that he compelled his owne hand which had written those blasphemies to be the instrument to punish him, & that in his braine, which had devised the same.[18]

Suicide and despair, then, were commonly allotted an important place in God's retribution for sin but, on turning to the main body of Jacobean drama, one notices something rather remarkable. The punishment of evil-doers frequently takes the form of a despairing conscience or a shameful suicide but rarely are the two combined. When an evil character kills himself it is a 'desperate act' which will undoubtedly damn him, but it is not preceded by the outbursts of an afflicted conscience one might expect. Conversely, the many tyrants whose last speeches are filled with fearful references to guilt and damnation invariably fall by the swords of others, not their own. The traditional and powerful connection of suicide and despair is fragmented, though both are used in a broadly similar way to strike down the sinner. The explanation for this peculiarity lies, I am convinced, in the dramatists' awareness of the many redemptive connotations of suicide that existed *even within the Christian tradition of suicide as despair*. There was considerable danger of entangling the intended 'negative', retributive effect of a despairing death with more 'positive' feelings. An afflicted conscience, expressed in the conventional terminology of despair, was to some degree a sign of repentance and, if followed by an onstage suicide, would show a genuine contrition, theologically as valueless as that of Judas, but capable of winning audience sympathy. Moreover, a suicidal despair might suggest the original Morality pattern, the average or even good man (Redcross Knight) tempted and tested to the edge of destruction that he might eventually find salvation. It is the strength of many of the greatest plays of the period (beginning with *Doctor Faustus*) that the ambiguities of despair and suicide are *not* avoided. But when evil is to be punished such ambiguity could be fatal to the dramatic design and hence it is carefully shunned.

To come to specific examples, it was a particularly strong convention that tyrants and unbelievers should be attacked by conscience some time before their bloody end. When Richard III, after the ghosts of his victims have told him to 'despair, and die!', exclaims,

> O coward conscience, how dost thou afflict me!
> (V.iii. 180)

and later on in the same speech,

> I shall despair. There is no creature loves me;
> And if I die, no soul will pity me.
> (V.iii. 201-2)

it is natural to feel that this is Shakespeare's method of creating a brief moment of sympathy for Richard. Indeed, if Richard were actually to kill himself at this point, the spark of sympathy might be fanned into a warm glow. In fact the lines are primarily there to demonstrate that no man, even a 'bloody dog' like Richard, is beyond reach of the sting of remorse. Shakespeare, whose interests at that time were historical rather than tragical—the divided state rather than the divided mind—makes less of Richard's despair than the nearly contemporary *True Tragedy of Richard III*.[19] Nevertheless, such despair is a traditional part of the tyrant's role and the audience would feel cheated if it were absent. The tradition was as much theological and historical as dramatic. Burton gives long lists of examples in his section on the causes of despair:

> Tragical examples in this kind are too familiar and common; Adrian, Galba, Nero, Otho, Vitellius, Caracalla, were in such horror of conscience for their offences committed, murders, rapes, extortions, injuries, that they were weary of their lives, and could get nobody to kill them... Why had Richard the Third such fearful dreams, saith Polydore, but for his frequent murders? Why was Herod so tortured in his mind? Because he had made away Mariamne his wife. Why was Theodoric, the King of the Goths, so suspicious, and so affrighted with a fish head alone, but that he had murdered Symmachus and Boethius, his son-in-law, those worthy Romans?[20]

The repeated use of particular images and phrases defined the despair of tyrants and atheists as a specifically religious despair—a fear of damnation. There is a remarkable continuity of expression so that the terror of Domitian in Massinger's *The Roman Actor* (1626) is virtually indistinguishable from that of Richard III (c.1593). Both men, for instance, eloquently express the idea that the evil man is his own worst enemy, that evil is a form of self-destruction:

Richard: What do I fear? Myself? There's none else by.
              Richard loves Richard; that is, I am I.
              Is there a murderer here? No. Yes, I am:
              Then fly. What, from myself? Great reason why,—
              Lest I revenge. What, myself upon myself?
                                  (V.iii. 183–7)

Caesar: Presumptuous traytor thou shalt dye. What traytor?
              He that hath beene a traytor to himselfe
              And stands convicted heere. Yet who can sit
              A competent Judge ore *Caesar*? *Caesar*. Yes
              Caesar by *Caesar*'s sentenc'd, and must suffer.
                                    (V.i. 193–7)

The inherent power of the 'guilty conscience' convention when handled by a writer of genius is shown by the Cardinal's brief flicker of fear in *The Duchess of Malfi*. This cold, ruthless, and worldly churchman is not beyond the reach of the mental torment with which the wicked were traditionally punished:

I am puzzled in a question about hell:
He says, in hell there's one material fire,
And yet it shall not burn all men alike.
Lay him by:—how tedious is a guilty conscience!
When I look into the fish-ponds, in my garden,
Methinks I see a thing, arm'd with a rake
That seems to strike at me.
                          (V.v. 1–7)

In the security and seclusion of a rich man's garden, a homely gardening implement is terrifyingly transformed into the kind of instrument used by fiends to drag the damned down into the pit. A familiar dramatic situation has been infused with a new terror. Likewise, in the delusion of Ferdinand that he is a wolf, Webster is able to imply guilt and remorse 'through the traditional beliefs that wolves disclose murders by digging up the victims and that those suffering from Lycanthropia have wolf's hair under the skin like the hair shirts of penitents',[21] without resorting to the already stereotyped terminology of despair. For, like all useful dramatic conventions, the sinner's attack of conscience was used so often that it was gradually drained of power and meaning. It is difficult to avoid the feeling in the later drama that the playwrights are 'going through the motions' when they attach these outbursts to their characters. Ferrand, King of Naples, in Fletcher and Massinger's *The Double Marriage* (1619–23) is a cruel tyrant and must be quickly defined as such for the audience. So, on his first appearance, he suddenly tells the other characters to 'Be Statues without motion [or] voice', 'while [I] tell my troubles to my self.' This is the remarkably crude staging preliminary to a conscience-stricken soliloquy:

> When I was innocent;
> I yet remember I could eat and sleep,
> Walk unaffrighted, but now terrible to others:
> My guards cannot keep fear from me
> It still pursues me; Oh! my wounded conscience,
> The Bed I would rest in, is stuft with thorns;
> The grounds strew'd o'r with adders, and with aspicks
> Wher e'r I set my foot.
>   (I.i. Cam.VI, p.332)

It is hardly necessary to add that nothing in Ferrand's subsequent behaviour shows a vestige of 'that scrupulous thing styl'd conscience'.

Conscience, like despair, has a double significance. It is the means by which man is woken from sinful security to repentance, but it may also act as an evil angel and wake him to despair. The primary sin of tyrant figures is their presumption. They often explicitly deny the power of conscience to reach them:

Rollo: Conscience, *Latorch*, what's that?
Latorch: A fear they tye up fools in: natures coward,
             Pauling the bloud and chilling the full spirits
             With apprehension of meere clouds and shadowes.
Rollo: I know no conscience, nor I feare no shadowes.[22]

Later, of course, like the Macbeths, he endures 'nightly dreames of death and horrour', for it was thought to be part of God's scheme of retribution that such men *should* suffer the pangs of conscience yet not truly repent. Their hardened hearts are to be touched by the lance of Penitence, but never to break with contrition. They despair but they never kill themselves since dramatically, if not theologically, such a death is all too apt a symbol of contrition.

Looking at the matter from the other side, we find that when evil characters in the drama *do* kill themselves (which, as I have shown earlier, is in many respects the most fitting way for them to die), their suicide is usually not preceded by the sort of conscience-stricken speeches I have quoted. Frequently, indeed, such deaths take place offstage, the most effective way for a dramatist to strip them of either redemptive or heroic connotations. Shakespeare's practice in this matter is especially illuminating. Whilst Othello, Brutus, Antony, Cleopatra, Romeo, and Juliet kill themselves in full view of the audience, Goneril, Lady Macbeth, and the Queen in *Cymbeline* do so offstage,[23] and the exact circumstances of the deaths of the latter two are left open to doubt. The curt presentation of the end of Goneril and Regan allows Shakespeare to say exactly what he wants to say, and no more. When Kent tells Lear,

> Your eldest daughters have fordone themselves,
> And desperately are dead.
>
> (V.ii. 292–3)

it becomes irrevelant which was the murderer and which the suicide. The idea of repentance is excluded and we are left with a general image of the self-destructiveness of evil. The retribution that evil brings on itself is the only lesson to be drawn from their deaths:

> This judgment of the heavens, that makes us tremble,
> Touches us not with pity.
>
> (V.iii. 232–3)

In a similarly brief and effective manner, Fletcher and Massinger dispose of the wicked mother, Brunhalt, in *Thierry and Theodoret*. She chokes herself offstage, thus solving the problem of how to punish her. This problem is raised more explicitly in Beaumont and Fletcher's *Cupid's Revenge* (c.1607–12), when Leucippus has to decide what to do with his malignant stepmother Bacha. His decision is,

Leave her to heaven brave Cousen,
They shall tell her how she has sind against em,
My hand shall never be staind with such base bloud:
Live wicked Mother,
That reverent title bee your pardon, for
I will use no extremitie against you,
But leave you to heaven.

                                        (V.iv. 150–6)

A few lines later, Bacha acts out the 'judgment of the heavens' by killing herself, though not before she has stabbed Leucippus.

It is apparent, I think, that the convention of suicide as a punishment for sin had to be carefully handled, but was particularly useful as a means of disposing of female criminals, who could not so readily be killed in battle or single combat in the manner of their male counterparts. Blood was generally repaid by blood in the drama, and suicide was the most obvious way of removing 'a woman dipp'd in blood' from the stage. Thus Edmund can be killed in a semi-judicial combat, but Goneril and Regan must destroy themselves. Macbeth can 'try the last' on the field of battle, but his wife's punishment is through her own 'violent hands'. The fundamental point I am making, however, remains the same whether a man or woman is involved. If such a suicide is given more than the briefest treatment, it tends to evoke a more complex response than a simple recognition of the retributive aspect, the 'judgment of the heavens'. Thus Levidulcia in *The Atheist's Tragedy* and Evadne in *The Maid's Tragedy* are allowed a measure of repentance that partially redeems them and invests their deaths with a certain honour; and in the three plays which I shall conclude this chapter by discussing, *The Changeling, Women Beware Women*, and *Macbeth*, the relation of suicide to the theme of retribution is not as straightforward as might appear.

The dominant theme of Middleton's two great tragedies can be summed up by lines from one of his less successful plays, *Hengist, King of Kent*:

                    See, sin needs
        No other destruction than [what] it breeds
        In its own bosom.

                                        (V.ii. 76–8)

Middleton is concerned with the pattern of retribution rather than that of redemption and this retribution is worked out within the terms of this world. His sinners destroy themselves; they do not need overtly divine intervention to help them on their way. Nor, in *The Changeling*, do they even need the intervention of the human revenger who so frequently acts as God's scourge of sin. Tomazo de Piracquo, brother of the murdered Alonzo, wanders through the play demanding revenge, but his revenge is achieved through no act of his own. Dramatically redundant in one sense, he serves to symbolise the kind of play Middleton did *not* choose to write. Middleton's conception was 'that revenge should not come from an outside force, the revenger of blood, but should result from the mutual destruction of the criminals.'[24] This conception is carried out in the final scene of the play (which is usually attributed to Middleton's co-author William Rowley) when De Flores fatally wounds Beatrice-Joanna before stabbing himself. Clearly, the main function of their deaths is to dramatise the spiritual suicide they have already committed and to make explicit the inevitable punishment they have incurred.

According to Una Ellis-Fermor, Middleton's characters 'do not redeem themselves in death; their deaths are of a piece with their lives and become them no better.'[25] Much of the writing in the last scene upholds this view. The final and fatal meeting of De Flores and Beatrice is rendered sordid and devoid of any aura of love tragedy by Alsemero's comments as they 'couple' in his closet:

> I'll be your pander now; rehearse again
> Your scene of lust, that you may be perfect
> When you shall come to act it to the black audience
> Where howls and gnashings shall be music to you.
> (V.iii. 114–17)

More poetically, Rowley modifies a familiar and potent image to suggest Beatrice's total damnation. She tells her father,

> I am that of your blood was taken from you
> For your better health; look no more upon't,
> But cast it to the ground regardlessly:
> Let the common sewer take it from distinction.
> (V.iii. 150-3)

Frequently in the drama, dying characters refer to their polluted blood (often with the double meaning of 'lust') as flowing from their wounds for their 'better health'. For example, Beaumelle in Massinger and Field's *The Fatal Dowry* says, after being stabbed by Charalois,

> I approve his sentence,
> And kisse the executioner: my lust
> Is now run from me in that blood, in which
> It was begot and nourish'd.
>
> (IV.iv. 151-4)

Beatrice, however, cannot be redeemed by a beneficial bloodletting. *She herself* is the polluted blood that must be thrown into the common sewer, as the corpses of medieval suicides sometimes were. It is an image of devastatingly non-redemptive finality, and its meaning is confirmed by the way all the other characters onstage ignore her dying plea for forgiveness (which of course tells us something about them as well as about her).

The manner of her death does not significantly modify the play's pattern of retribution, but what of De Flores, whose suicide should complete the same pattern? To a large extent it does, of course, but, as I have suggested, when the suicide of a sinner is treated more than cursorily it ceases to function solely as a symbol of retribution. De Flores' final speeches undeniably introduce the idea of a love tragedy:

> here's my penknife still.
> It is but one thread more, [*stabs himself*]—and now 'tis cut.
> Make haste, Joanna, by that token to thee:
> Canst not forget, so lately put in mind,
> I would not go to leave thee far behind.
>
> (V.iii. 173-7)

This does not redeem De Flores in Christian terms; he himself recognises that he and Beatrice 'are left in hell'; but we are forced to re-examine our assumptions about their relationship. It has been not unusual to regard Beatrice as a relative innocent, corrupted by the villainous De Flores. Thus, in Empson's influential analysis of the play, De Flores is the goblin who snatches a child-like Beatrice into his world and changes her to something like himself.[26] Yet, from the beginning, Beatrice is shown to be morally defective, incapable of recognising the significance of any situation. It is she who is responsible for the murder, she who is 'the deed's creature'. In contrast, De Flores sees all too clearly that money will not 'buy a capcase' for his conscience, and that the price of enjoying Beatrice is damnation. Without illusions about her, he can still love her: 'I lov'd this woman in spite of her heart' (V.iii. 165). In fact his suicide (the ultimate gesture of the devoted lover) serves to remind us that he has given 'all for love', consciously damned himself for a woman he knows to be worthless. Like Conrad's *Heart of Darkness*, the play develops a contrast between a self-aware, unillusioned kind of evil and a blind, self-deluding variety. In both works there is a deliberate element of moral paradox in the suggestion that De Flores and Kurtz are in some way more admirable than Beatrice and the Congo 'pilgrims', who commit crimes hardly knowing what they do. In *The Changeling*, the moral paradox is most directly expressed in the assertive theatricality of De Flores's love-suicide. His self-destruction becomes much more than a simple image of guilt and punishment.

Women Beware Women has been seen as an extension of Middleton's early comedies of intrigue:

> The energetic competitiveness of the intrigue in which dog eats dog and rogue bilks rogue need only be pushed a little further, made a matter of life and death, and the delicate net of plot and counterplot becomes a web of mutual destruction.[27]

For two-thirds of the play we have been presented with a group of highly individualised characters gradually coarsening and hardening as they become embroiled in sin. If Middleton had continued to write in naturalistic terms we might have had a particularly black comedy of spiritual self-destruction. Instead, the characters suddenly turn murderous and all perish in a highly symbolic fatal masque. The sudden change of manner is unsettling and the introduction of the Cardinal in Act IV, like the final masque, is a reversion to a more conventional representation of the punishment sin entails. His speeches repeat in other-worldly terms what has already been demonstrated within the confines of the play's action. Once he has spoken, a sentence of death hangs over all the characters and, whatever its failings, the masque functions satisfactorily as a symbol of 'the inevitable result of the spiritual suicide of lust and ambition'.[28] The ironical aspect of retribution looms large as Guardiano is impaled on his own spike, and Livia, who acted as bawd to Hippolito and Isabella, is poisoned while playing the role of Marriage Goddess. Amidst what is really a mass suicide, two of the characters literally kill themselves. Is the presentation of their deaths intended to do more than make us tremble at heaven's fatal judgement on them? Hippolito, after being mortally wounded by poisoned arrows fired by the cupids (an ironic reminder of his incestuous passion for Isabella), has a long speech before running his breast against one of the guards' swords. He says that

> man's understanding
> Is riper at his fall than all his lifetime.
> (V.ii. 152–3)

and explains how the various deaths are the direct consequence of 'lust and forgetfulness'. He analyses both the causes and the mechanism of the retribution that has fallen on them, before seeking, not a lover's death, but the end to an intolerable and shameful pain (the 'wild flame' of both poison and incest that runs through his blood). His death is 'of a piece' with his life and with Middleton's scheme of crime and punishment.

Bianca's suicide is another matter, however. After the poisoned drink she prepared for the Cardinal has been accidentally swallowed by her lover the Duke, she attempts to suck death from his lips before seizing the poisoned cup and drinking from it. In one sense, her manner of death completes the image of inner and outer deformity with which she described herself immediately after her seduction by the Duke:

> Yet since mine honour's leprous, why should I
> Preserve that fair that caused the leprosy?
> Come poison all at once.
>
> (II.ii. 424–6)

After a literal poison has eaten into her face, she echoes these lines quite closely:

> But my deformity in spirit's more foul—
> A blemished face best fits a leprous soul.
> (V.ii. 204–5)

The ironic pattern of retribution is clear enough here, but the two moments when she actually attempts suicide (the kiss and the drink) are heavy with other implications. The poisoned (or otherwise deadly) kiss was a powerful and frequently used dramatic convention with a wide range of meaning. At one extreme we have the lecherous Duke in *The Revenger's Tragedy* kissing the skull of Gloriana (*Duke*: 'O, 't has poisoned me.'/ *Vindice*: 'Didst not know that till now?' (III.v. 152–3)), and at the other, Juliet seeking a 'restorative' from dead Romeo's lips, a means to rejoin her lover. *Both* connotations are present in Bianca's kiss of death:

> Thus, thus, reward thy murderer, and turn death
> Into a parting kiss. My soul stands ready at my lips,
> E'en vexed to stay one minute after thee.
> (V.ii. 195–7)

Sin finds its reward of death whilst at the same time the lover's soul is freed from its bodily prison. In the same way, the 'poisoned chalice' of 'even-handed justice' which she raises to her lips is metamorphosed into a loving-cup which she has shared with the Duke:

> Pride, greatness, honours, beauty, youth, ambition,
> You must all down together, there's no help for't.
> Yet this my gladness is, that I remove,
> Tasting the same death in a cup of love.
> (V.ii. 218–21)

Like Claudius, she is 'justly served', but Middleton also uses the act of suicide to remind us of the earlier Bianca who gave up fortune and family to marry for love. The reminder is particularly ironic since now the object of her devoted love is another man, the man who destroyed her original innocence. She dies in order to accompany the serpent to another paradise. Undoubtedly

Middleton relished the irony of this, but, with its admixture of romantic sympathy, it is a more complex kind of irony than the harshly didactic reversals with which he so often punishes his characters. The ambiguity of the moment creates a small disturbance within the overly-neat scheme of retribution, the kind of disturbance all plays need if they are to avoid becoming diagrams.

Macbeth has been called 'a study in fear'[29] and the fear which is referred to is the traditional terror of the guilty conscience. 'When we set aside the fear of God, a mere nothing fills us with trepidation.'[30] One function of the many images of darkness which fill the play is to suggest continually that time of day when a despairing conscience is most active, an idea that received its most eloquent expression in Nashe's *The Terrors of the Night*:

> Even as when a condemned man is put into a darke dungeon, secluded from all comfort of light or companie, he doth nothing but despairfully call to minde his graceless former life, and the brutish outrages and misdemeanours that have throwne him into that desolate horrour; so when Night in her rustie dungeon hath imprisoned our ey-sight, and that we are shut seperatly in our chambers from resort, the divell keepeth his audit in our sin-guilty consciences.[31]

Macbeth's punishment begins the very moment after Duncan's murder with his inability to say 'Amen' to the prayer 'God bless us'; such an inability to pray was one of the traditional features of despair ('he that lieth in sinnes against his conscience, cannot call upon the name of God').[32] The imagined voice crying 'Sleep no more! Macbeth does murder sleep' simultaneously expresses both his crime and his punishment. In murdering the sleeping Duncan, Macbeth also destroyed his own 'innocent sleep' and, shaken by 'terrible dreams', will share the fate contrived by the witches for the sailor journeying to Aleppo: 'Sleep shall neither night nor day/ Hang upon his penthouse lid' (I.iii. 19–20).

It is the way we are forced to participate in this suffering that allows Macbeth to remain a sympathetic figure despite his crimes, a dramatic manipulation which is closely linked to the paradoxes of despair. For Macbeth's mental torment does not simply signify the kind of punishment thought appropriate to tyrants in the drama but, as the sign of a still operative conscience, is an important part of what defines him as a man, as 'one of us'. The concept 'man', in relation to both gender and species, is subjected to intense scrutiny throughout the play, from the disturbing androgyny of the witches when they first appear to Macbeth and Banquo, to the death of Young Siward in the final battle ('like a man he died'). The clear implication throughout is that the definition of manliness utilised by Lady Macbeth and gradually accepted by Macbeth himself excludes elements essential to full humanity. Thus in the Banquet scene, Macbeth's quite natural terror when confronted by Banquo's ghost provokes the taunt 'Are you a man?', helping us to understand why he should celebrate the inhuman hardening of his sensibility with the ironic claim 'I am a man again'. The hallucinations and terrible dreams which initially tormented him, although marks of guilt and despair, were also marks of humanity and marks of an active conscience, signifying the possibility of repentance. It is when he *ceases* to suffer in this way that he is most certainly damned. By the time Birnam Wood comes to Dunsinane, he has supped so full of horrors that he has 'almost forgot the taste of fears'. His conscience is now seared up, his heart hardened. Beyond the fear of God, he is also beyond the mercy of God for 'He that is without feare, is without hope'.[33] He has reached a state of soul in which conscience is so dead that the conventional guilt and fear of the after-life experienced by the despairing wicked have been replaced by a more general sense of meaninglessness and hopelessness, a feeling beyond normal religious despair. It is the leaden passage of days 'To-morrow, and to-morrow, and to-morrow' within 'recorded time' rather than the horrors of eternity which weighs upon Macbeth at the last. Because Shakespeare's presentation of this process is so intimate, we never lose dramatic sympathy with the protagonist, yet undoubtedly some loss of humanity is signified. The courage which Macbeth still has left is only the courage of the desperate animal:

> They have tied me to a stake. I cannot fly,
> But bear-like I must fight the course.
>
> (V.vii. 1–2)

It is Shakespeare's intention to make us feel this loss of humanity as if it were our own, to bind us forcibly to Macbeth's experience without allowing us the luxury of thinking him redeemed in any respect, the luxury of evading our close implication with damnation.

It should be clear now, in terms of my overall argument, why, despite the self-destructive nature of his actions (the Porter's 'farmer that hanged himself on th'expectation of plenty' is surely an image for Macbeth himself), Shakespeare deprives Macbeth of any urge to kill himself.

> Why should I play the Roman fool and die
> On mine own sword? Whiles I see lives, the gashes
> Do better upon them.
>
> (V.iii. 1–3)

Suicide would, in two separate ways, reconstruct Macbeth as a man, allow us to feel more positive about him than suits the play's purpose. A Roman death would have heroic, 'manly' implications that Shakespeare wished to avoid, and, even if considered as an act of despair, would emblematise the workings of a conscience which no longer exists. Macbeth has reached a state beyond even the remorse of Judas.

That a suicidal despair arising from a guilty conscience might have a humanising as well as retributive significance is surely apparent from the way Lady Macbeth is presented. In the first scene in which she appears, she performs a terrifying act of self-damnation in calling upon the powers of darkness to dehumanise her. Whether actually demoniacally 'possessed' or not, she succeeds during the first half of the play in achieving a murderous strength of purpose which could be called inhuman. The dramatic difficulty of getting an audience to share fully in the fate of such a character is overcome by presenting the guilt-ridden distraction of the sleep-walking scene and suggesting its likely end in suicide ('Therein the patient/ Must minister to himself'). Rather than just being marks of an inevitable punishment, the suffering of the sleep-walking scene and the subsequent suicide represent her suppressed humanity reasserting itself in the form of conscience. They are the crucial means by which we are forced to recognise her as 'as one of us' and are prevented from turning aside with the dismissive judgement 'fiend-like'. Yet any increase of dramatic sympathy is rigorously controlled so as not to produce an impression of salvation at the last. Her anguish and her suicide are not finally redemptive because there is no real sign of repentance in them. The language of her distraction shows obsession with her sin rather than sorrow for it, and her suicide is prevented from becoming a really powerful dramatic image of contrition by being relegated to a doubtful offstage occurrence, reported by the scornful Malcolm.

Although the dramatic progression is different in each case, Macbeth's heart gradually hardening while his wife's is breaking, the overall intention remains the same—to force the audience into maximum identification with the protagonists without relaxing in any way the assumption that they are indeed damned. There is a determination not to let us, the audience, off this particular hook but to make us recognise, by means of a forced experience of damnation, that there are dark potentialities in each one of us. For a moment, in the English scene, it appears that even the virtuous Malcolm is a reservoir for every evil known to mankind and, when Lady Macbeth has finished her obsessive hand-washing, the Doctor's comment is 'God, God forgive us all!'. In striving to present the Macbeths as both human and damned, Shakespeare was closely aware that the despair and suicide of the wicked might have more than just retributive implications.

CHAPTER 3

Temptation and Affliction

here I understond, the tribulacions by which the devyll thorow
the suffraunce of god, eyther by hym selfe or other that are his
instruments, temptith good folke to impacience as he did Job.
(Sir Thomas More)

The pattern of retribution discussed in the last chapter was a
relatively late development of suicide's darker connotations. The
Christian classification of suicide as an act of despair originally
found expression in a rather different pattern—the pattern of
temptation. From the Patristic period to the Reformation the
most usual conception of desperate self-murder was as a
temptation of the devil[1] rather than 'a judgement and
punishment of some notable sinnes'. For the Middle Ages, the
most typical suicidal figure was the monk or ascetic tempted
beyond endurance by the wiles of Satan. Rather than the epitome
of a life of sin, suicide was a particularly dangerous temptation for
the godly—an idea that has a neat parallel in the conception that
melancholy tended to afflict noble and intelligent natures. It
is in the Book 'Of Temptation' that Caesarius records most
of his examples of suicides in *The Dialogue on Miracles*, and
it is as a 'horrible temptacion' which spiritual comfort is
needed to combat that More classifies suicide in *A Dialogue
of Comfort against Tribulation*. It is as the ultimate threat to
the average or good man, rather than the inevitable end of the
evil man that suicide and despair appear in the early Morality
plays.

The fundamental pattern of the medieval Moralities was a fall
into sin of the Mankind figure followed by repentance and
forgiveness. The temptations of Lust, Greed, and so on are
almost always successful since man is a fallen creature: in

Hooker's phrase, 'all flesh is guilty'. To succumb to these temptations is not inevitably damnable, but to succumb to the final temptation of despair (usually symbolised by suicide) is to deny the power of grace and damn both body and soul. The lapse into despair of the Mankind figure is one of the crucial moments in these dramas of salvation, since it is the point when the hero is closest to damnation.

> The greatest danger for mankind in the moralities is not falling into sin (for all men sin) or yet in delaying repentance (for that can be amended), but in despairing of the possibility of the forgiveness of one's sins.[2]

Because the pattern of the early Moralities is one of redemption rather than final damnation, comfort is always at hand when a man falls into a potentially damnable despair. The rustic hero of *Mankind* is prevented from hanging himself by Mercy. Manhood, after his name has become Age, is saved from suicide by Perseverance, the brother of Conscience, in the play *Mundus et Infans*. When Magnificence, ruined by his bad advisers, is visited by Despair and Mischief in Skelton's political Morality, Good Hope intervenes to save him. This sequence of sin, despair, comfort, and redemption is maintained in non-dramatic allegorical literature such as *Piers Plowman*[3] and *The Faerie Queene*, but in the later Moralities begins to be modified by a Calvinist emphasis on reprobation. In a play like *The Tyde Taryeth No Man* the two patterns coexist. Greediness is persuaded to kill himself by Despair, but Wastefulness is saved from a similar fate through the comfort of Faithful Few. The two endings of Woodes' *The Conflict of Conscience* represent a wavering on the part of the author between the Calvinist desire to make an 'awful warning' out of a real-life case of apostasy, and the older, Catholic ritual of comfort and repentance. At the end of *Doctor Faustus*, Marlowe reproduces the familiar tableau of the hero brought to the brink of suicide by his despair but saved by an agent of comfort and repentance. However, although the Old Man prevents Faustus from killing himself with the dagger Mephostophilis hands him, Faustus's repentance immediately shifts from God to Lucifer when he is threatened by Mephostophilis:

Mephostophilis:	Thou traitor, Faustus, I arrest thy soul
	For disobedience to my sovereign Lord:
	Revolt, or I'll in piecemeal tear thy flesh.
Faustus:	I do repent I e'er offended him.
	Sweet Mephostophilis, entreat thy Lord
	To pardon my unjust presumption,
	And with my blood again I will confirm
	The former vow I made to Lucifer.
	(xviii. 77–81)

The full power of this scene is dependent on an awareness of its ironic reversal of the older pattern of temptation, comfort, and redemption.

As the drama grew more secular, it ceased to have so much use for a pattern that reached completion only in the after-life. Jacobean tragedies focus more on death than rebirth, more on retribution than redemption, though the underlying religious assumptions are frequently similar. However, as Marlowe showed in *Doctor Faustus*, the inherited conventions of dramas of repentance could be twisted to produce great tragedy. There were two main ways in which the traditional Morality play influenced the professional Elizabethan playwrights, and through them the Jacobeans:

> In the ultimate sense it provided the inherited mythic idea of a theatrical treatise on the human condition... In the direct sense, however, the morality play appeared to the Elizabethans as a set of traditional stage conventions of plot and character that could be put to many useful and contemporary theatrical purposes in the emerging popular drama.[4]

The particular climactic image of the older drama—mankind poised between comfort and despair—had a secure niche in the Jacobean imagination. At the end of *The English Traveller* (1621–33), Heywood merges his characters into the archetypal pattern:

Wife:	Oh tell me if thy name be Geraldine,
	Thy very lookes will kill mee?
Dalavill:	View me well,
	I am no such man; see, I am Dalavill.

Wife: Th'art then a Devill, that presents before mee
            My horrid sins; perswades me to dispaire;
            When hee like a good Angel sent from Heaven,
            Besought me of repentance.
                              (V.i. vol.IV, p.92)

Massinger achieves a similar effect in *A New Way to Pay Old Debts* (1625) when, early on in the play, Sir Giles Overreach plots to destroy Welborne spiritually as well as materially. He tells his 'creature', Marrall,

> Doe any thing to worke him to despaire,
> And 'tis thy Masterpeece.
>   (II.i. 66–7)

When Marrall meets up with Welborne, he tries to persuade him to hang or drown himself but is confidently rebuffed:

> 'Twill not do, deare tempter,
> With all the Rhetorike the fiend hath taught you.
> I am as farre as thou art from despaire.
>   (II.i. 120–3)

Whatever our previous doubts about Welborne's character, this little episode establishes him as an erring but redeemable Mankind figure, rather than a hardened sinner. He is subject to temptation and has in fact descended to wastefulness and riotousness, but he is capable of resisting the only finally damning temptation, that of despair and suicide. By contrast, Overreach and Marrall are confirmed as unmitigatedly evil, in terms of the Morality pattern, literally agents of the devil.

In *Antonio and Mellida* (1599–1600), Marston gives us a more secular, and characteristically individual reworking of the ritual of despair and comfort. After Mellida has failed to keep a rendezvous, Antonio petulantly resolves to kill himself: 'Spite of you all, I can and I will die' (III.iii. 192). His next few lines contain some powerful images of death and despair. Like Job, he curses his birth; like the Duchess of Malfi, he uses the image of the thousand ways that lead to death to imply suicide; like Lear, he uses the fact that we come crying into the world to symbolise man's misery. Nevertheless, Feliche's response makes it clear that

we are to regard this outburst as childish. Feliche calls him
'perverse' and 'peevish' and finds a singularly pragmatic way of
preventing his suicide:

> If you'll be peevish, by this light I'll swear
> Thou rail'dst upon thy love before thou diedst
> And call'd her strumpet.
>
> (III.ii. 216–18)

This succeeds in 'comforting' Antonio, who goes off quoting (in
Italian) a proverb about Hope living in spite of Fate. In the Stoic
terms of the play, it is Antonio's manly dignity rather than his
soul which has been endangered by despair. Feliche is able to save
him not by exhortations to look up to heaven, but by a threat to
his earthly fame (that his 'dead trunk' will be 'held in vile regard').

As these examples show, the critical moment for mankind in
the Moralities—the temptation to despair and suicide—could be
incorporated into the later secular drama as a significant figure of
speech or the basis for a short scene. A more fundamental use of
this situation was hindered, I believe, by its openly religious and
other-worldly significance. The redemptive implications of the
sequence of temptation, despair, and comfort looked beyond the
deaths which concluded a Jacobean tragedy and, with the
strength of longstanding ritual, imposed an orthodox Christian
meaning which a dramatist might not wish to stress so heavily.
On the other hand, of course, a piece of Christian propaganda like
Massinger's *The Renegado* (1624) could make full and
uncomplicated use of the tried and tested formula. The sub-plot
of this play concerns a pirate,

> the shame of *Venice* and the scorn
> Of all good men: The perjurde *Renegado*
> *Antonio Grimaldy.*
>
> (I.i. 105–7)

who attacks Christian ships on the orders of the Turks. When he
falls into disfavour with his Turkish masters he is reduced to
poverty and despair. He enters 'in rags', talks of his overwhelming
guilt and how he dare not 'looke upward', and plans to kill
himself.[5] A Jesuit priest, Francisco, fulfils the role of 'Mercy' or

'Comfort', and gradually wins him away from his suicidal despair
by an act of ritual forgiveness. He is able to signify his repentance
not by killing himself but by performing the good work of
rescuing the characters in the main plot from a martyr's death. To
a mind like Massinger's, steeped in the sentiments and images of
an orthodox faith, the most natural dramatic use of suicide was in
the context of a temptation to final despair which must be
overcome. More than any Jacobean dramatist, Massinger relies
on the Morality formula since it harmonises with the openly
Christian outlook of so many of his plays. Thus, in *The Virgin
Martyr* (written with Dekker), the final temptation that both
Dorothea and the converted Theophilus face before their
martyrdom is that of despair.[6] To gain salvation, they must go to
death willingly but not voluntarily—a peculiarly Christian
distinction.

Believe as you List is set in Roman times, but Massinger
illustrates his theme of Stoic constancy in the face of suffering
with a powerful, if anachronistic, version of the traditional
temptation scene.[7] Antiochus, the dispossessed King of Lower
Asia, has been wandering from court to court trying to achieve
recognition of his rights. Roman policy, enacted by the brutal
Flaminius, has thwarted him and eventually he falls into the hands
of the Romans. In the prison at Callipolis, Flaminius tries to
make him admit he is an impostor. For Antiochus to deny his
identity would be like selling his soul, and the devilish nature of
Flaminius is emphasised by the role of tempter he assumes:

> since I had hym in
> my power I have usd all possible meanes that might
> force hym into despaire & soe to doe
> a violence on hym selfe.
>
> (IV.i. 76–9)

A Jailer presents Antiochus with a poniard and halter, in the
traditional manner of the devil's agents. He immediately grasps
their significance and, as he has just made a speech desiring death,
one might expect him to 'ease the burthen of a wretched life'.
However, he reacts in a very *Christian* manner by viewing suicide
as hell's attempt to ensnare his soul:

>   my better angell
> though wantinge power to alter fate discovers
> their hellishe purposes. yes, yes, 'tis soe.
> my bodies death will not suffice, they aimde at
> my soules perdition, and shall I to shun
> a few howers more of miserie betray her?
>   (IV.ii. 55–60)

The ritualistic nature of the scene is underlined by the entry *'above'* of the three Romans, Flaminius, Metellus, and Sempronius, at the moment when Antiochus discovers the rope and dagger. As Lucifer, Beelzebub, and Mephostophilis gathered to watch the final despair of Faustus, these human agents of hell come to mark how Antiochus 'doth demean himself' in the most crucial situation a man can face.[8]

The long scene of Antiochus's testing uses the traditional concept of suicide as a damnable temptation to illustrate the idea that

>   affliction
> Expresseth virtue, fully, whether true,
> Or else adulterate.[9]

The physical humiliation of the ex-king (at one stage he is reduced to a galley-slave, and enters with his *'head shaved'*) and the mental torture of despair never finally destroy his 'constancy'. The temptation scene shows him grappling with despair and winning a spiritual victory by overcoming it. The idea that affliction has a spiritual value has been put forward many times in art, religion, and philosophy to help explain and mitigate the miseries of the human condition. It has its roots in both Christian and classical thought, which partly explains why the central scene of the old religious drama can perform a similar structural function in a play about Stoic values.

In *Shakespeare and Christian Doctrine*, R. M. Frye tried to confine this idea to pagan thought by pointing out that only Christ's suffering had redemptive value in the Christian scheme of salvation. To assume that the individual's noble endurance of pain atoned for his sins was, according to Luther, to 'deny God and his Christ, blaspheme his grace and pervert his gospel.'[10] In fact, as I shall show, it is possible to quote Christian sources (including Luther) as well as pagan ones in support of the value of suffering and, particularly, the value of despair. It is in *this* sense that the temptation to suicide plays its most impressive role in the Jacobean drama, and transcends a purely Christian significance: as a species of affliction which 'tests' the protagonist and expresses his or her virtue as much by the testing as by the outcome.

The standard biblical example of this is Job, whose story seems especially designed to allay the doubts that arise when a good man is seen to be afflicted by the devil and tempted to impatience. Everything happens through God's permission, we are told, and by suffering even to despair, Job eventually wins grace. Looked at in these terms, despair is not the mark of damnation but a means to salvation the godly must undergo. 'God's best servants, and dearest children have been so visited and tried',[11] for 'whom he loveth, him he chasteneth: whom he exalteth, he casteth down: whom he saveth, he damneth first. He bringeth no man to heaven, except he send him to hell first.'[12] The 'hell' referred to in the last quotation is the state of despair and of course the relevant theological distinction is between temporal and final despair. To undergo a loss of hope, equal perhaps in its intensity to final despair, and emerge safely from such an experience was an important, even necessary stage in the journey towards grace, corresponding to the perceived value of suffering in general. 'So that affliction is a school or academy, wherein the best scholars are prepared to the commencements of the Deity.'[13]

As well as Job, the other main examples of the holy nature of temporal despair were David, the apostle Peter, and Christ himself. Luther considered the experience of despair so essential to the pattern of a holy life that he insisted, contrary to Catholic doctrine, that Christ's sufferings on the cross had been spiritually as well as physically identical to the extremities of human suffering. 'Just like us, Jesus on his cross touched the depths of despair, believed himself forsaken by God. This was for Luther the real meaning of his "descent into hell".'[14] Luther himself had experienced such a 'descent into hell', and through it had achieved his 'saving' insight that human righteousness could accomplish nothing:

I myself. . . have been offended more than once even to the abyss of despair, nay so far as even to wish that I had not been born a man: that is before I knew how beautiful that despair was, and how near o Grace.[15]

For both Catholic and Protestant, much of the value of despair for sinful humans was to wake them from the slothful sleep of security (referred to as 'mortals' chiefest enemy' by Hecate in one of the interpolated scenes of *Macbeth*). Only by being made painfully aware of his frailty, as Peter was when the cock crowed, could a man avoid the sin of presumption. If suicide does not follow, 'he shall have in conclucion greate cause to be glad of this fall.'[16] Before entering the House of Holiness it is necessary for Spenser's Redcross Knight to pass through the Cave of Despair with all its attendant dangers. It is the ultimate paradox of despair that it should be a crucial stage in the achievement of holiness.

All this was implicit in the pattern of the medieval Moralities, but the emphasis there fell on the outcome of the temptation to despair rather than on the experience of that temptation. One or two of the greatest Jacobean tragedies make use of this inherited pattern to explore the experience of despair. Because the specific dramatic situation we are discussing, the temptation to desperate suicide, was a convention of the religious drama, and because conclusions about the paradoxical value of experiencing such a temptation correspond to a fundamental Christian attitude, it might be natural to assume that the 'Cliffs of Dover' episode in *King Lear* and Ferdinand's torment of the Duchess in *The Duchess of Malfi* can be interpreted in an orthodox Christian manner. It would be quite wrong to ignore the Christian implications, but as I noted when discussing *Believe as you List*, doctrines about the value of affliction are also firmly rooted in pagan ethics. In the most famous line in the *Agamemnon*, Aeschylus says that Zeus 'hath stablished as a fixed ordinance that "wisdom cometh by suffering".'[17]

Superficially similar is the Stoic view that the world's ills are a device of Providence to try the fortitude of a brave man: 'Fire tests gold, misfortune brave men.'[18] In fact, the Stoic idea of the good man's heart being hardened into indifference by calamity differs considerably from the Aeschylean and Christian concept of wisdom entering through a broken heart. Often in the drama, it is a purely Stoic interpretation of affliction that is expressed, as in the praise for the dead Sophonisba which concludes Marston's tragedy:

> Thou whom like sparkling steele the strokes of Chance
> Made hard and firme; and like wild fier turnd
> The more cold fate, more bright thy vertue burnd.
>   (V.iii.vol.II, p.63)

In the greatest plays, however, Christian and classical implications are mingled, just as they are in so many of the drama's suicides. Moreover, it would be truer to say that inherited beliefs about the value of affliction form the basis for dramatic *explorations* rather than dramatic affirmations. With this in mind, I want to turn to *King Lear* and *The Duchess of Malfi* to see how Shakespeare and Webster use the traditional scene of despair and comfort as part of a wider statement about suffering and evil.

The 'Cliffs of Dover' episode is perhaps the most obvious of the many Morality elements in *King Lear*. From the very first line 'When shall I come to th'top of that same hill?' with its hint at the Mountain of Purgatory, the stylised nature of Gloucester's attempt at suicide forces us into an allegorical interpretation of his fall and recovery. Just in case any member of the audience is slow to grasp what is happening, Edgar explains the whole scene in an aside:

> Why I do trifle thus with his despair
> Is done to cure it.
>   (IV.vi. 33–4)

This equates Gloucester's misery with the Christian sin of despair, and makes clear that Edgar will assume the role of 'Comfort' or 'Mercy'. As he revives his father, Edgar pretends that the figure who led him to the cliff's edge 'was some fiend'. Gloucester must be somehow convinced that his attempted suicide was not the natural response to his situation, but the effect of diabolic temptation. By also being convinced that his life's 'a miracle', he can be brought to 'bear affliction'. Sometimes miracles are needed before a thing can be believed (as was both claimed and disputed during this period in relation to Christianity as a whole). When the King of France is told of Cordelia's loss of favour, he says that to believe her guilty of a monstrous offence 'Must be a faith that reason without miracle/ Should never plant in me' (I.i. 222-3). In Gloucester's current predicament, it is impossible to reason him into a belief that the gods really care for him. Only a providential miracle will suffice, and Edgar manufactures one. Without resorting to the obvious anachronisms of a Massinger, Shakespeare is able to suggest by the overall structure of the scene and some carefully chosen details that Gloucester's pagan despair can be assimilated into the Christian pattern of salvation. Although 'For the stock stage emblems of despair, the rope and the dagger, Shakespeare has substituted a cliff's edge of the mind',[19] the debt to the Morality tradition is obvious. Gloucester's despair, through the paradox mentioned above, has a value independent of its outcome. It teaches him compassion for Poor Tom and enables him to 'see more clearly', even as his ordinary sight is destroyed. Yet when this despair leads to suicide, the broadly tragic implication that 'wisdom cometh by suffering' is modified by a formal scene of comfort and hope, with ineradicable Christian associations. Given the close parallelism of sub-plot and main plot, it is natural to enquire how far this Christian pattern modifies the play as a whole.

Like Gloucester's, Lear's suffering has an Aeschylean value and, like Gloucester's, a darker, non-redemptive side. Whereas Gloucester's despair turned to suicide, Lear's sinks into madness. Once more, the wronged child acts as agent of comfort to the despairing father. Cordelia takes Lear out of the grave and unbinds him from his wheel of fire. The scene of his recovery is directly parallel to Edgar's salvation of Gloucester, but is presented in a more personal, less formalised manner, though still including such traditional elements as a symbolic change of clothing. The Morality pattern is completed again, but this time only to be shattered. In the holocaust of the last Act, the agent of comfort is herself hanged, with the additional and horrible irony that her murderers intended

> To lay the blame upon her own despair
> That she fordid herself.
> (V.iii. 255-6)

In the play *Mankind*, the hanging of the comforter had been an evil dream inspired by the devil. Here it is actualised. Lear, restored to life and hope by Cordelia, is plunged into a new and life-hating despair.

> Vex not his ghost. O let him pass! He hates him
> That would upon the rack of this tough world
> Stretch him out longer.
>
> (V.iii. 314–16)

It seems to me of considerable significance that these words of Kent's are in reply to Edgar's 'Look up, my Lord', a phrase used time and again in the drama as a counsel of hope to those in despair of salvation. By means of this one highly charged expression, Shakespeare is able to suggest that Edgar is carrying over his role of comforter into the main plot. Kent's reply tells us that the time for such comfort is past. Edgar may have saved his father from despair and suicide, but such a formally Christian outcome is impossible here. We have moved from Morality to tragedy.

Reconsidering the Edgar-Gloucester scenes in the light of this, we find that they are not, perhaps, so straightforward after all. It is not enough to say that the stylised form of the 'Cliffs of Dover' episode connects it with older dramatic parables of despair and comfort, which symbolised a universal pattern of truth. It also has to be recognised that everything in this scene is an illusion: there is no cliff and no seashore, no diabolic temptation and no fall. There is no 'miracle' at all, but only an act of human kindness. The gods do not appear (as Jupiter does in *Cymbeline*). The only visible sign of something *more*, something beyond the human, would be the stars which were probably painted on the underside of the Globe's stage covering; and the stars—as will appear from *The Duchess of Malfi*—are a notoriously ambiguous symbol, signifying everything and nothing. The identification of religious comfort with illusion occurs unemphatically but pointedly in the lines with which Edgar assures Gloucester that he has indeed fallen from a great height.

Gloucester: But have I fall'n, or no?
Edgar: From the dread summit of this chalky bourn.

> Look up a-height. The shrill-gorged lark so far
> Cannot be seen or heard. Do but look up.
>
> (IV.vi. ·56–9)

The classic advice to the despairing, 'Look up', becomes part of the deception designed to establish the reality of the cliff. Obviously one can relate this to Edgar's later attempt to get Lear to look up in his dying moments.

The 'Cliffs of Dover' scene is not the first time in the play that a non-realistic dramatic technique has been used to project an important 'truth', whilst simultaneously undermining that truth by means of the obvious deception involved in its presentation. Edgar's unlikely disguise as Poor Tom is a way of inserting into the play a powerful dramatic image of man as only 'a poor, bare, forked animal'. This degraded being, corresponding to Calvin's view of man as 'a worm of five feet long', has all the appearance of an 'essence', 'the thing itself', a core of reality reached by removing all the trappings of civilisation, a process which began when Lear took off his crown. Yet to Lear's anguished question 'Is man no more than this?' the answer is of course both literally and symbolically 'yes', since we remain aware that this 'essence' is the disguised and kindly Edgar. The play never dismisses the reality of human kindness, and Edgar's care for his father is the one thing which *is* real in the 'Cliffs of Dover' scene. However, a further consideration of the scene will help explain why such kindness may not be enough.

In the Morality plays, the temptation to despair and suicide such as Gloucester undergoes in Act IV, scene vi was a truly climactic episode. The protagonist was brought to hope only after a real experience of the abyss. It seems at first that this scene does represent such an experience. After telling the Old Man that 'Thy comforts can do me no good at all', Gloucester is brought by Edgar to 'within a foot/ Of th'extreme verge'. Surely, when he leaps over that edge, we shall have reached a *ne plus ultra* of suffering and any hope which follows will have a firm foundation in its full knowledge of the worst. But the cliff does not exist, 'th'extreme verge' is not there, and the play continues to exemplify Edgar's dictum 'The worst is not/ So long as we can say "This is the worst"' (IV.i. 27–8). Each apparent low point is succeeded by a moment of hope, before a further and deeper plunge—a pattern which is far more painful than an unmitigated series of disasters would be. The despair and recovery of Gloucester is instantly followed by the 'side-piercing sight' of the mad Lear. The loss of the battle is mitigated by Albany's moral stand, but then his hopes for Cordelia ('The gods defend her!') are immediately answered by the entry of Lear with Cordelia in his arms. Only in the last scene of all is 'th'extreme verge' reached, and by then there will be no use for Edgar's comfort.

Moreover, if one looks more closely at the nature of Gloucester's recovery, it is much less complete than the Morality pattern would lead one to expect. When Gloucester cries out to the gods,

> Let not my worser spirit tempt me again
> To die before you please.
>
> (IV.vi. 214–15)

he is accepting Edgar's and Christianity's view of the situation and the phrase 'worser spirit' deliberately invokes Morality associations. Yet Gloucester is never brought to hope, only to endure. After Lear's forces have been defeated he seeks death again, and this time Edgar's comfort does not take the form of a providential miracle but is merely a piece of unadorned Stoicism:

> Men must endure
> Their going hence, even as their coming hither;
> Ripeness is all.
>
> (V.ii. 9–11)

A few lines earlier, Edgar had promised, 'If ever I return to you again,/ I'll bring you comfort', but all he can now offer is 'Ripeness is all'. Gloucester's reply 'And that's true too' seems to suggest a multiplicity of truths, a whole series of explanations of the world and its sufferings. The Christian answer, exemplified by Edgar and Cordelia, that despair is succeeded by comfort has its place in the play, but it is not the final place. The 'Cliffs of Dover' episode re-enacts a conventional situation in order to tell us part of the truth, but not all of it. It tells us that comfort is always at hand, but the play in its entirety tells us that comfort is not always enough. In the end we are reduced to the bedrock of tragedy—that the price of wisdom is suffering, and such a price may not be worth paying.

Webster's *Duchess of Malfi* also explores the value of affliction, both through the implications of its action and the explicit pronouncements of its characters. As they part for the last time, Antonio and the Duchess give respectively a Stoic and a Christian version of this doctrine:

Antonio:	Make patience a noble fortitude,
	And think not how unkindly we are us'd:
	Man, like to cassia, is prov'd best, being bruis'd.
Duchess:	Must I, like to a slave-born Russian,
	Account it praise to suffer tyranny?
	And yet, O Heaven, thy heavy hand is in't.
	I have seen my little boy oft scourge his top
	And compar'd myself to't: naught made me e'er
	Go right but heaven's scourge-stick.

(III.v. 73–81)

The testing of the Duchess, the 'proving' of her virtue, occurs in Act IV in the prison scenes, and it takes place in the context of Ferdinand's admission that the purpose of the various torments is 'To bring her to despair' (IV.i. 116). The pinnacle of Webster's tragic achievement is a re-working of an old formula. Before she enters heaven's gates on her knees, the Duchess, like the Redcross Knight before his entry into the House of Holiness, must overcome the linked temptations of pride and despair. As usual, suicide is one of the symbols of this damning despair, and it is interesting to note that Ferdinand, her diabolical persecutor in Act IV, twice before in the play presents the Duchess with a dagger, in the manner of a personified Despair figure. Although Ferdinand does not explain his gesture on either occasion, the second time it occurs it is explained for us. The Duchess shows Antonio the poniard:

Antonio:	ha, what means this?
Duchess:	He left this with me:-
Antonio:	And it seems did wish
	You would use it on yourself?
Duchess:	His action seem'd
	To intend so much.

(III.ii. 149–52)[20]

The later episodes in the prison—the dead man's hand, the waxwork statues and the masque of madmen—are continuations of what was implied by the offer of the dagger. Bosola's first words to the Duchess in Act IV, the conventional greeting 'All comfort to your grace', and her reply, 'I will have none', prepare us for the religious significance of the succeeding torments. After seeing '*the artificial figures of Antonio and his children, appearing as if they were dead*', the Duchess succumbs to the temptation of despair and wishes to kill herself:

Bosola: Come, you must live.
Duchess: That's the greatest torture souls feel in hell—
              In hell: that they must live, and cannot die.
              Portia, I'll new-kindle thy coals again,
              And revive the rare and almost dead example
              Of a loving wife.
Bosola: O fie! despair? remember
              You are a Christian.
Duchess: The church enjoins fasting:
              I'll starve myself to death.
Bosola: Leave this vain sorrow:
                              (IV.i. 69–76)

By one of Webster's most extraordinary ironies, Ferdinand's agent and the Duchess's murderer, Bosola, is the man who fulfils the traditional role of Comfort and saves the Duchess from suicide and despair, even as he carries out the orders of his devilish master. Webster demonstrates 'that a man can be at once an agent of God and of the Devil. Bosola torments the Duchess yet comforts her, destroys yet saves her.'[21] When he tells her, 'Come, be of comfort, I will save your life' (IV.i. 86), his words are, if taken in a physical sense, a 'cruel lie' or at best a good intent that perishes by the wayside. Yet in spiritual terms he does indeed save her life. When he finally has her strangled, he has brought her to a Christian acceptance of death that is free from the despair of 'I'll starve myself to death' and the opposite danger of pride and security implied in her heroic assertion 'I am Duchess of Malfi still'.

The ambiguities of Bosola's role are nowhere clearer than in the following exchange:

Duchess: I'll go pray: no,

```
                  I'll go curse:-
Bosola:               O fie!
Duchess:                      I could curse the stars.
Bosola:                              O fearful!
Duchess:      And those three smiling seasons of the year
              Into a Russian winter, nay the world
              To its first chaos.
Bosola:                      Look you, the stars shine still.
                                      (IV.i. 95–100)
```

This last line

> has often been taken, as by F.L. Lucas, to express 'the insignifi-
> cance of human agony before the impassive universe'. But it is also
> a further attempt to strengthen the Duchess in her suffering; an
> affirmation of faith in the divine order which still exists, undis-
> turbed by the chaos around her. In this one great line Bosola's
> double role is epitomised.[22]

Webster's likely source for the line (a quotation by Montaigne
from Pliny the Elder) supports the former interpretation.
'There is no such societie betweene heaven and us, that by our
destinie the shining of the starres should be as mortall as we
are.'[23] Yet one can also see in it the traditional advice to those
in despair—to look up to heaven and find mercy. It is Bosola's
tragedy that he can offer this comfort to the Duchess but not
partake of it himself, as Antonio has told him earlier:

> You would look up to heaven, but I think
> The devil, that rules i' th'air, stands in your light.
> (II. i. 94–5)[24]

Bosola's strange, self-divided stance (noted by Ferdinand in his
remark 'Thy pity is nothing of kin to thee') adds a new dimension
to the familiar scene of temptation and comfort, but I believe the
fundamental significance of the episode remains primarily
Christian, a belief which finds confirmation in the remainder of
Act IV. Almost immediately after the Duchess's cursing of the
stars, Ferdinand admits that he is trying to bring her to despair,
and recognises Bosola's desire to comfort her soul. Bosola tells
him that

> when you send me next,
> The business shall be comfort.
>   (IV.i. 136–7)

and adopts the highly significant disguises of tomb-maker and
bellman. In these roles[25] he is able to remind her of her mortality
and cure her of that sickness which is the more dangerous for
being insensible—security, the converse of despair and, as Bosola
mentions later, sometimes called 'the suburbs of hell'. By a
medieval insistence on the frailty of the body and earthly titles,
Bosola completes his partly unconscious role of spiritual guide
and brings the Duchess to heaven on her knees.

Act IV of *The Duchess of Malfi* is the most brilliant Jacobean
version of the ritual of despair and comfort enacted in the older
drama, and it follows through the ritual to the Christian
conclusion of a 'good death'.

> But this is not to make Christianity the *raison d'être* of the play.
> We may trace the success of *The Duchess* to this adoption of
> Christianity as a dramatic formula but this is not necessarily to
> call Webster's play a Christian drama.[26]

Like Edgar's salvation of Gloucester, the scenes between Bosola
and the Duchess are episodes in a play, not the play itself. The tide
of violence in Act V washes over the pattern we have traced and
leaves it at best blurred, at worst obliterated. Certainly, the
madness and despair which overtake Ferdinand and the Cardinal
have an ironic inevitability which is amenable to a Christian
interpretation, but the miserable death of Antonio at the hands
of the man who intended to save him adds an 'absurd' dimension
to the action ('Such a mistake as I have often seen/ In a play') and
defies rationalisation.[27] The Echo scene carefully establishes that
the Duchess's influence persists beyond the grave, but then that
influence is shown to be powerless to alter events. Antonio
ignores the Echo's warning and goes to his death.

Bosola is deeply moved by the Duchess's noble suffering and
turns against his former masters, but only after he has been
refused the reward for her murder. In what way the events of Act
IV 'explain' or influence the rest of the play is left in doubt. Like

Shakespeare in *King Lear*, Webster has set up a traditional pattern of meaningful suffering, of despair and redemption, whose meaning is then thrown into question by what follows. Is to 'look up' in the play to find heaven, or only to have 'a miserable knowledge of the small compass of our prison'? Against the assurance of the Duchess ('your able strength/ Must pull down heaven upon me'), we have to set the desperate, post-Reformation confusion of the Third Madman's cry, 'Greek is turned Turk; we are only to be saved by the Helvetian [i.e. Genevan] translation' (IV.ii. 91–2).

What is not in doubt is the nobility of the Duchess's suffering, the manner in which she 'gives a majesty to adversity'. Her specifically Christian confrontation with despair also has a more general tragic value, and this is possibly Webster's main reason for adopting an ancient and not particularly fashionable dramatic formula. Such a formula gave him immediate access to the idea that 'affliction expresseth virtue fully' for it is true that 'the virtues which he admired and which called forth the supreme effort of his genius flowered only in the darkness of mortal agony'.[28] In a traditional test to destruction, the temporal despair which 'may befal the best of God's children', Webster found his means of expressing virtue fully. But whether the suffering and death of the Duchess points to anything beyond itself is something 'we may go read in the stars', the stars which shone down on her torment.

> *Ferdinand:*   Why some
> Hold opinion, all things are written there.
> *Bosola:*   Yes, if we could find spectacles to read them.
> (III.i. 60–2)

CHAPTER 4

Repentance, Expiation, and Honour

For sinne and shame are ever tyed together,
With Gordi[a]n knots, of such a strong threed spun,
They cannot without violence be undone.
(Webster)

To some degree linked with the paradox that despair may be the
first step to redemption is the idea of suicide as a form of
repentance and expiation for sin. As I have mentioned, one of the
main arguments proving the damnability of suicide was the fact
that 'the very sin doth preclude all ordinary ways of repentance'.[1]
Yet even orthodox theologians admitted that the act might
involve a measure of penitence. The general opinion concerning Judas was that he had been repentant, but that his manner
of repentance had been, in Calvin's phrase, 'nothing better
than a kind of threshold to hell'.[2] Thomas Aquinas put it as
follows:

> And this penitence was not true penitence: however it possessed
> something of penitence: for penitence must be a mean between
> hope and fear: Judas indeed had fear and sorrow because he
> lamented his past sin; but he did not have hope. And such is the
> penitence of the wicked.[3]

Nevertheless, in the course of attacking Catholic teaching on
repentance, Calvin was able to claim that Judas had fulfilled all
the Catholic requirements for a true repentance because, 'in Judas
there was perfect contrition of heart, confession of the mouth,
and satisfaction for the money', and centuries before, Origen had
held that this repentance might have been sufficient to redeem
him.[4]

77

The strange interrelationship of despair, suicide, and repentance lies at the heart of Marlowe's *Doctor Faustus*. The general tendency of the play is to balance despair against repentance in a thoroughly traditional way ('I do repent and yet I do despair'); the despair Faustus suffers is the consequence of a failure to repent. Yet in the long and crucial speech where suicide is firmly wedded to despair (vi. 18–32), there is an opposite implication. After telling how the various means of suicide are laid before him in his moments of despair, Faustus continues,

> And long ere this I should have done the deed
> Had not sweet pleasure conquer'd deep despair.
> Have not I made blind Homer sing to me
> Of Alexander's love and Oenon's death?
> And hath not he, that built the walls of Thebes
> With ravishing sound of his melodious harp,
> Made music with my Mephostophilis?
> Why should I die, then, or basely despair?
> I am resolv'd, Faustus shall not repent.
> (vi. 24–32)

If the last two lines are considered closely, it becomes apparent that repentance is here being *associated* with, rather than opposed to, despair and suicide. Faustus saves himself from these by plunging, resolved and impenitent, into the 'vain pleasure of four and twenty years', but at the same time cuts himself off from the contrition that is so paradoxically close to despair. This pattern repeats itself at the climax of the play when Faustus nearly kills himself with the dagger provided by Mephostophilis. Although in the grip of a damnable despair, his penitence means that he is close to grace:

> I see an angel hovers o'er thy head
> And with a vial full of precious grace,
> Offers to pour the same into thy soul.
> (xviii. 61–3)

All he needs to do is 'call for mercy, and avoid despair'. Instead, however, he calls for Helen of Troy to be his paramour and damns himself irretrievably. 'Sweet pleasure' has temporarily conquered 'deep despair', but at the price of extinguishing a saving repentance.

The point I am making—that despair can be a form of repentance, and suicide an atonement for sin—is set forth with particular clarity in *Richard III*. Richard has accosted Lady Anne as she was accompanying the hearse of the murdered Henry VI:

> *Anne:* Fouler than heart can think thee, thou canst make
> No excuse current but to hang thyself.
> *Richard:* By such despair I should accuse myself.
> *Anne:* And by despairing shalt thou stand excusèd
> For doing worthy vengeance on thyself
> That didst unworthy slaughter upon others.
> (I.ii. 83–8)

In requiting a death with a death, Richard would 'stand excusèd' because he would have offered a complete 'satisfaction' for his sins and, as Leonora says in *The Devil's Law Case*,

> you know repentance
> Is nothing without satisfaction.
> (IV.ii. 301–2)

The idea of a full and perfect satisfaction for past crimes is present in some of the suicidal outbursts of Massinger's 'renegado', Antonio Grimaldi. Whereas his initial desire to drown himself had been merely a despairing attempt to hide from the 'heavy wrath of God', he progresses (if that is the word) toward the concept of a grisly atonement:

> Yet to finde peace within heere,
> Though all such as I have maim'd, and dismembred
> In drunken quarrells, or orecome with rage
> When they were giv'n up to my power, stood heere now
> And cride for restitution; to appease 'em,
> I would doe a bloody justice on my selfe;
> Pull out these eies that guided me to ravish
> Their sight from others; lop these legs that bore me
> To barbarous violence; with this hand cut off
> This instrument of wrong, till nought were left me
> But this poore bleeding limblesse truncke, which gladly
> I would divide among them.
> (IV.i. 61–72)

In fact this speech, which represents the penitent face of despair, occurs just before Grimaldi is spiritually healed by the Jesuit priest. Although damnable and 'Judas-like', the suicidal justice he contemplates is perhaps a first step towards a spiritual recovery (or rather, a second step, since his initial despair represented a rejection of the blasphemy and irreligion of his former life).

The suicide of Levidulcia in *The Atheist's Tragedy* mingles despair and repentance to achieve 'the kind of sentimental melodrama in which Jacobean audiences delighted'.[5] In the overall structure of the play, Levidulcia stands for the bestial, unreasoning side of D'Amville's 'naturalism'. Whereas D'Amville's reason is corrupted at its source by his atheism, and his sins are those of the intellect, Levidulcia's greatest sin, like Vittoria's in *The White Devil*, lies in her blood, and her blood must pay for it. When she sees her husband and lover kill each other for her sake, the evil consequences of lust are brought home to her. After a long final speech, which typifies the whole play in its combination of cardboard characterisation, black-and-white morality, and carefully wrought imagery spiced with word-play, she stabs herself to death. Her last words are important evidence in any assessment of her death:

> O, in their wounds
> I feel my honour wounded to the death.
> Shall I outlive my honour? Must my life
> Be made the world's example? Since it must,
> Then thus in detestation of my deed,
> To make th'example move more forcibly
> To virtue, thus I seal it with a death
> As full of horror as my life of sin. *Stabs herself*
> (IV.v. 79–86)

The reference to her death as 'full of horror' supports the interpretation that she has died in damnable despair and is destined to become an exhibit in the theatre of God's judgements. However, there are other points to consider. Her suicide could be seen as illustrating an idea expressed by Heraclide, in Nashe's *The Unfortunate Traveller*. After being ravished by Esdras of Granado, she proclaims before stabbing herself,

The onely repeale we have from Gods undefinite chastisement, is to chastise our selves in this world: and I will, nought but death be my pennance, gracious and acceptable maie it be: my hand and my knife shall manumit mee out of the horrour of minde I endure.[6]

This establishes that the suicide of a woman who thought of herself as dishonoured could be presented as an overtly Christian form of penance, and indeed a penance necessary to secure eternal life. In fact, Levidulcia's suicide seems to me to function primarily as an atonement for the bloodshed she has caused and as a means of letting forth the 'blood' of her passion which had overwhelmed her reason. It is a mark of repentance, not of further sin, and is parallel to D'Amville's attack of conscience in the graveyard scene, which, despite being a form of despair, is the nearest he comes to salvation. Unlike Levidulcia, whose penance is enacted before her purpose cools, D'Amville slips back into a state of complacent security, which is more certainly fatal to his soul than any act of self-punishment could have been.

The most obviously Christian suicide in any of these plays is that of Anne Frankford in Heywood's *A Woman Killed with Kindness* (1603). There is little tension between despair and repentance since everyone in the play, including Anne herself, considers her decision to starve herself to death as totally justified within the Christian ethic. The normal Christian association of suicide with despair makes one brief appearance in Frankford's words to Wendoll, the friend who took advantage of his hospitality to commit adultery with his wife.

> Go, to thy friend
> A Judas; pray, pray, lest I live to see
> Thee Judas-like, hang'd on an elder tree.
> (xiii. 75–7)

Interestingly enough, Wendoll, the villain, shows no inclination to kill himself but, on the contrary, shows a worldly love of life and resilience of conscience. In his last speech he compares himself to Cain, who must wander the world carrying his burden of sin, but concludes brightly,

When I have recovered, and by travel
Gotten those perfect tongues, and that these rumours
May in their height abate, I will return:'
And I divine (however now dejected)
My worth and parts being by some great man prais'd,
At my return I may in court be rais'd.

(xvi. 131–6)

His unrepentant life-wish is intended by Heywood as a guilty contrast to the holy and penitent suicide of Mistress Frankford. Her death is partly a matter of recovering her wifely honour and, in the immediate aftermath of the shameful discovery, she seems to look on her 'honour' as something distinct from her soul's salvation:

Nay, to whip but this scandal out, I would hazard
The rich and dear redemption of my soul.
He cannot be so base as to forgive me,
Nor I so shameless to accept his pardon.

(xiii. 137–40)

This is a temporary aberration, however, and the rest of the play unites honour and salvation as the twin benefits she will gain from death. In fact, through a constant reiteration of terms with Christian significance, it is her soul's salvation that dominates the last few pages of the play and secular honour and shame are quietly consumed in a greater flame. The difficulty in presenting her suicide as an essentially Christian and penitent act is largely overcome by the form of her death—self-starvation. Although religious fasting was supposed to stop short of death, its objectives corresponded exactly to Anne's intentions:

The thirde ende [of a fast] is, to testifie the humilitie and contrition of our hearts, that is to say, our inward sorrow and
grief for sinne, and our repentance and effectuall turning unto
God. The fourth end of a fast, is to admonish us of our guiltines
before the Lord.[7]

Moreover, there is little doubt that many of the revered ascetics of the early Church were virtual suicides who hastened their own death through fasting and penances.[8] No other form of self-inflicted death could so successfully establish Anne Frankford as an explicitly Christian example of contrition and repentance.[9]

A similar domestic tragedy by Heywood, *The English Traveller*, also ends with the guilty wife desiring death to show her repentance:

> swell sicke Heart,
> Even till thou burst the ribs that bound thee in;
> So, there's one string crackt, flow, and flow high,
> Even till thy blood distill out of mine eyes,
> To witnesse my great sorrow.
>
> (V.i.vol.VI, p.92)

In this case, the overtones of despair that attend a normal suicide are banished, not by the Christian associations of fasting, but by a 'natural' death from a broken heart. The wife's death is the only adequate means of atonement but it must be untainted with despair. At the root of these contradictions is the very essence of Christianity—Christ's voluntary death in atonement for the sins of mankind. In Christian dogma, of course, the death of Jesus was sufficient satisfaction for all sins, and salvation is achieved through faith in its grace, not by imitating its voluntary nature. Nevertheless, the idea that voluntary death atones for sin has an emotional force in Christian thought which leaps over the careful categories of theology, allowing a sense of value to emerge by association rather than logic. Poetically and metaphorically an expiatory suicide can be an imitation of Christ as well as of Judas. That Mistress Frankford should redeem herself from sin by her death is a strictly untheological notion, yet there is no more obviously Christian play in the entire period than *A Woman Killed with Kindness*. As K.O. Myrick said while discussing the problem of suicide in Shakespeare's plays, 'The religious implications of tragedy are mingled with literary conventions, and are to be found not in a literal and pedantic piety, but in poetic suggestion to our hearts and imagination.'[10]

Sometimes in harmony with Christian notions of atonement and repentance, and sometimes working against them, is the classically derived concept of gentlemanly honour. From Aristotle and Cicero, Renaissance moral philosophers developed a system of ethics which stressed the importance of 'reputation', the social recognition of virtue, in a manner quite foreign to Christian teaching. In doing this, they were formalising and systematising military and aristocratic traditions of honour which had coexisted with Christianity throughout the Middle Ages. The emphasis of a death for honour falls more on 'satisfaction' and the avoidance of shame than on contrition and remorse. One who aspires to the title of gentleman 'maketh choise rather to die, then dishonour his life with reproch', an attitude which sounds more classical than Christian.[11] In works of moral philosophy, the conflict with Christian values is played down by the adoption of a form of words which always carefully avoids a direct advocacy of suicide. In the theatre, there is a freer mingling of value systems in the presentation of expiatory suicides.

One might think that the Christian elements of such a death would be most prominent in those plays with a Christian setting, but this is not necessarily so at all. In Fletcher and Massinger's *Sir John van Olden Barnavelt* (1619), one of the conspirators, Leidenberch, is persuaded by Barnavelt to kill himself in prison as expiation for confessing part of the plot, and to prevent further confessions being extorted from him. Barnavelt's persuasion is couched in terms of fame and credit rather than the Christian imagery of blood washing away the stain of sin:

> he that looses
> his Creadit (deere as life) through doubt, or faintnes
> is guilty of a doble death, his Name dies,
> he is onely pious, that preserves his heire
> his hono^r, when he's dead.

> (III.iv. 1546–50)

This predominantly classical tone is maintained by Leidenberch himself. His repentance is elevated to a soldierly, heroic level by being placed in the context of the famous Roman suicides. He calls on

> Thou soule of *Cato*,
> and yo^u brave Romaine speritts, famous more
> for yor true resolutions on yor selves,
> then Conquest of the world.

> (III.vi. 1633–6)

to witness his death. One effect of this speech is to transmute the pathetic realities of a piece of recent history into art. While remaining true to the known details (the use of a penknife and the presence of Leidenberch's son), Fletcher[12] is able to give a heroic dimension to an act of despair in a prison cell. When Barnavelt pronounces the final epitaph on Leidenberch, 'he was a weak man indeed: but he has redeemd it' (IV.iii. 2026), the redemption refers more to honour and reputation in this world than the after-life, for which Anne Frankford's suicide was a necessary preparation.[13]

By contrast, plays dealing with the pre-Christian period sometimes infuse a repentant death with (anachronistic) Christian associations. The dying words of the disgraced Roman general Penyus in Fletcher's *Bonduca* seem to embrace both a secular and a divine atonement:

> My soul I give to heaven, my fault to justice
> Which I have done upon my self.
> (IV.iii. 169–70)

These lines come towards the end of a scene in which Fletcher has contrasted and analysed through a debate between two characters the differing Christian and classical notions of mercy, justice, and repentance. Petillius has been sent to Penyus to dissuade him from the suicide it is feared will follow his shameful action in refusing to send help to Swetonius. In his official role of 'comforter', Petillius mouths a number of stock Christian sentiments. He speaks of the blackest sins as being 'washed white again' if a man earnestly seeks forgiveness. Meanwhile Penyus stands firm in regarding himself as beyond pardon:

> *Petillius:* Is there no medicine called Sweet mercie?
> *Penyus:*   None, *Petillius;*
> There is no mercie in mankinde can reach me,
> Nor is it fit it should; I have sinn'd beyond it.
> *Petillius:* Forgivenesse meets with all faults.
> *Penyus:*   'Tis all faults,
> All sins I can commit, to be forgiven:
> 'Tis losse of whole man in me, my discretion
> To be so stupid, to arrive at pardon.
> (IV.iii. 80–6)

The major irony of this stage of the argument is that both the audience and Penyus know that Petillius is putting on an act. Earlier Petillius had said, half aside, that Penyus, whom he had found prone on the floor, must either be dead or about to kill himself:

> It cannot be he dare out-live this fortune:
> He must die, 'tis most necessary; men expect it;
> And thought of life in him, goes beyond coward.
> ...he's certain dead,
> Or strongly means it; he's no Souldier else,
> No Romane in him.
>   (IV.iii. 37–48)

All Petillius's talk of forgiveness has been a sham and 'out of character' and is present in the scene simply to stir up interest in a problem of honour. Within the Roman framework of the play, Petillius has acted as devil's advocate in suggesting that disgrace can be atoned for without suicide. He eventually admits that he thinks Penyus should die and compresses the whole debate on Christian and pagan ethics into a neat paradox when he says scornfully,

>   and certain
> There is a mercy for each fault, if tamely
> A man will take't upon conditions.
>   (IV.iii. 126–8)

We are certainly meant to admire Penyus's decision to kill himself and to see it as a necessary expiation for his fault, 'a way to make all even'. Nevertheless, there is a final twist to the argument when Petillius refers to 'my sin', after Penyus has killed himself. The implication is that although the suicide is to be commended it should not have been urged.[14] The overall effect of this scene—and of many others in the Beaumont and Fletcher canon—is of an external discussion and refinement of ethical problems rather than a depiction of the inner life of a character. Despair, atonement, and forgiveness are shuffled and realigned during the argument till a satisfactory conclusion is reached. Penyus's death is a successful motion in a debate rather than a personal tragedy.

Other plays in which a repentant suicide is related to ideas of honour and satisfaction are Massinger's *A Very Woman* (1634) and Beaumont and Fletcher's *The Maid's Tragedy* (1608–11). In the former play, Cardenes, a suitor to Almira, dishonourably provokes a duel with his rejected rival Antonio, the Prince of Tarent. Badly wounded, he is also plunged into despair as he comes to recognise the baseness of his behaviour:

> I am a beast, the wildest of all beasts,
> And like a beast I make my blood my master.
> 　　　　　　　　　　　(III.iii. 23–4)

In a similar manner to Francisco's cure of Grimaldi in *The Renegado*, the doctor, Paulo, attempts a spiritual regeneration of Cardenes. He presents a series of symbolic masques and appears to Cardenes in a number of different disguises, intended to win him from despair. In his first disguise, as a friar, he pretends that he himself committed a far worse sin than Cardenes but was able to find grace through a sincere repentance. This approach has an unfortunate effect when Cardenes decides that only one form of repentance can give sufficient satisfaction for his crime:

> 　　　Then in honor
> Wronging him so, I'll right him on my self:
> There's honor, justice, and full satisfaction
> Equally tender'd; 'tis resolv'd, I'll do't.
> 　　　　　　　　　　　(IV.ii. 106–9)

Before he can stab himself, he is disarmed. Repentance is not enough. Cardenes must learn that suicide is not a true sign of an honourable 'satisfaction'. In his next disguise as a soldier, Paulo redefines honour for his patient:

> 'Tis poor in grief for a wrong done to die,
> Honor to dare to live, and satisfie.
> 　　　　　　　　　　　(IV.ii. 151–2)

The whole play is geared to a reconciliation of Christian virtues with gentlemanly honour. When Cardenes meets up with Antonio, the man who defeated him in the duel, he demands 'satisfaction', as a gentleman would do, but the 'satisfaction' he seeks is to be forgiven. Thematically, the false honour which seeks out quarrels and duels is linked with the false honour which regards suicide as a legitimate means of atonement.[15] In this play, honour is ultimately defined in orthodox Christian terms.

No such straightforward interpretation is possible when considering Evadne's suicide at the end of *The Maid's Tragedy*. It is a final, ambivalent variation on the shifting concepts of honour that run through the play. The basic plot rests on a peculiarly deformed notion of honour. Evadne marries Amintor in order to legitimise the consequences of her relationship with the King.

> I must have one
> To father children, and to beare the name
> Of husband to me, that my sinne may be
> More honorable.
>   (II.i. 15–18)

Amintor, who dishonoured his vows to Aspatia in order to obey the King, must either bear the dishonour of cuckoldry or stoop to the dishonour of a revenge against the King. Melantius knows that Amintor is too 'honest' to take this latter course, but when Evadne confesses the truth of her adultery to Melantius, he forces her to agree to kill the King as the only means of redeeming her shame. What is dishonourable for Amintor is apparently honourable for Evadne. She seems genuinely repentant and tells Amintor that she wants to atone for her sins:

> And never shall you see the foule *Evadne*
> Till she have tried all honoured meanes that may
> Set her in rest, and wash her staines away.
>   (IV.i. 278–80)

She appears to accept Melantius's view that murdering the King will help to cancel the shame of her adultery, but the audience is jolted by Amintor's shocked reaction to the murder into realising that this is another perversion of honour. As murder followed adultery, now suicide must follow murder and we are left to guess whether this represents a further deformity of ethics or a genuine contrition, 'a way to make all even'. In favour of the latter interpretation is the proximity of so many other noble suicides.

Aspatia has herself killed for love, Amintor stabs himself to express repentance as well as love, and Melantius intends to kill himself for a friendship that is indistinguishable from love. So when Evadne exclaims as she kills herself,

> *Amintor* thou shalt love me now againe,
> Go I am calme, farwell, and peace for ever.
> *Evadne* whom thou hatst will die for thee.
>   (V.iii. 169–71)

the overtones of love tragedy make it natural to associate her with the blessed company of martyrs for love. However, associations work in two directions, and possibly the main effect of the final scene is for Evadne's guilt to tarnish the honour of the other suicides: 'the juxtaposition of her suicide and Aspatia's points to the unconscious, morbid sexuality of Aspatia's death wish.'[16] In fact, the main impression one has of Evadne throughout the play is that of a damned soul, one who is incapable of a genuine repentance. She herself says,

> My whole life is so leaprous it infects
> All my repentance.
>   (IV.i. 196–7)

and Amintor tells her,

> Thou hast no intermission of thy sinnes,
> But all thy life is a continued ill.
>   (V.iii. 133–4)

She is in the familiar position of the blood-guilty revenger who has acted as Heaven's scourge in punishing the villainous King but who, like the scourge, must be thrown into the fire afterwards, thus allowing the dramatist to combine disapproval for revolutionary violence with a recognition of its inevitability in certain situations:

> for on lustfull Kings
> Unlookt for suddaine deaths from God are sent,
> But curst is he that is their instrument.
>   (V.iii. 293–5)

Like Judas, Evadne performed a necessary role, and like Judas the necessity provides no excuse. Her suicide is a form of repentance, in her view one of the 'honoured meanes' that will 'wash her staines away', but her repentance is infected and her death the reward of sin. As with her earlier behaviour in making use of Amintor as a showpiece husband, her 'honour' and her sin are inseparable. The ambiguity of her death is best summed up by her comment before her other act of 'repentance', her murder of the King:

> I have begun a slaughter on my honour,
> And I must end it there.
>
> (V.i. 23-4)

This can either mean that she will be continuing and completing the slaughter of her honour, or that she will be putting an end to it and redeeming herself. From such ambiguities derives the moral and psychological complexity of *The Maid's Tragedy*, the finest of all the 'Beaumont and Fletcher' plays.

The various themes of this chapter, repentance and despair, honour and shame, are all present in the death of Othello. As with the suicide of Penyus in *Bonduca*, religious implications of despair clash with a soldierly redemption of lost reputation. The conflict which Fletcher chose to express and resolve through an almost formal debate is more subtly located by Shakespeare in the very essence of Othello's character: he is both despairing sinner and noble soldier in his decision to stab himself. The ambiguities of his death have provoked considerable discussion, but in their eagerness to find a pattern of meaning in the play some critics have oversimplified and distorted the issues involved. The many words of Christian significance in the play (more than in any other Shakespeare play apart from *Richard III*) have encouraged an approach that finds a pattern of salvation or damnation in the life and death of Othello. Thus Irving Ribner confidently foresees a place in heaven for the hero:

> He dies in reunion with Desdemona, and in his expiation for his sin he merits divine mercy. In spite of the tortures of hell which Othello envisions for himself, the audience is assured of his eventual salvation.[17]

One doubts if the audience is assured of anything so definite. This is a 'Christian' reading of the play which goes against the many Christian images of damnation which cluster round Othello. Like Lady Macbeth, he formally and terribly renounces his gentler nature and turns himself into something inhuman:

> Arise, black vengeance, from the hollow hell!
> Yield up, O love, thy crown and hearted throne
> To tyrannous hate!
>
> (III.iii. 447–9)

When he finally learns the truth of Desdemona's innocence, he is as convinced of his own damnation as Faustus was. His conviction is expressed in the familiar obsession with hell that grips an afflicted conscience:

> When we shall meet at compt,
> This look of thine will hurl my soul from heaven,
> And fiends will snatch at it.
> ... Whip me, ye devils,
> From the possession of this heavenly sight!
> Blow me about in winds! roast me in sulphur!
> Wash me in steep-down gulfs of liquid fire!
>
> (V.ii. 274–81)

It is hard to see how the suicide of a Christian character who believes his soul as well as body has been ensnared can point to an assurance of salvation in Christian terms.

Seizing on this point, Paul N. Siegel and S.L. Bethell rush to the other extreme.[18] They expand the implications of the play's diabolic images to create a certainty of damnation. Siegel sees the whole play as a religious allegory and goes so far as to allot heaven or hell to the various minor characters (thus Roderigo is damned, Emilia and Cassio saved). He has an interesting comment on the textual alternatives 'Indian' or 'Judean' in Othello's final speech. If the Folio reading is accepted,

> 'Judean' would refer to Judas Iscariot, who, like Othello, killed himself in despair at his guilt and whose kiss of betrayal, bringing death to Christ, is recalled by Othello's words (V.ii. 359), 'I kiss'd thee ere I kill'd thee'.[19]

Recent scholarship strongly supports the reading 'Judean' and its
signifying of Judas, the only one of the twelve from the tribe of
Judah, and it seems highly probable that Shakespeare *did* intend
to associate Othello with Judas in his dying moments.[20] Such an
association would not of itself be definitive, however. It would be
one more image of despair to set against the suggestions of
redeemed honour, rather than a conclusive assertion that Othello
was damned. Moreover, I think the implications of Othello's
dying couplet,

> I kissed thee ere I killed thee. No way but this,
> Killing myself, to die upon a kiss.
>
> (V.ii. 358-9)

are broader than Siegel allows. Rather than suggest Judas
Iscariot, the dominant effect is surely to remind the audience
that Othello was 'one that loved not wisely, but too well', that
this is a tragedy of love as much as anything else and the
participants can be seen as tragic lovers rather than as murderer
and victim.

Both Siegel and Bethell regard Othello's suicide, because he is a
Christian in despair, as setting the seal on his damnation. Even
within the narrowly Christian terms of their approach this is open
to challenge:

> God...hath left no sufficient means to comprehend, and for
> that cause neither given any leave to search in particular who
> are infallibly the heirs of the kingdom of God, who castaways,
> ... And therefore Charity which 'hopeth all things', prayeth also
> for all men.'[21]

Certainty of damnation or salvation is not possible in this world
and without some such direction as '*the divells thrust him downe
and goe Triumphing*' (the stage direction at the end of Barnabe
Barnes's play, *The Devil's Charter*) is highly problematic in art.
This is a relatively minor objection however. The major weakness
in the arguments of Siegel and Bethell is that they rely too much
on schematically-applied theological dogma and overlook other
systems of value which are operative in the play. Whilst correctly
responding to the implications of Othello's visions of hell, they

ignore the greatness of his repentance and its association with a soldier's recovery of lost reputation. Similarly, Joan Ozark Holmer's more recent account of the theological implications of Othello's last speech is also weakened by her omission of any consideration of the secular values of honour and reputation which are being reasserted.[22]

Throughout the play reputation has been a major concern. Although Montano, the Governor of Cyprus, is a man of 'most allowed sufficiency', the Duke tells Othello to take over the defence of the island from him because 'opinion, a more sovereign mistress of effects, throws a more safer voice on you' (I. iii. 224-5). In a very direct expression of aristocratic and military values, Cassio speaks of his reputation, rather than his soul, as being 'the immortal part of myself' (II.iii. 253-4). The contradictory speeches on reputation which Iago makes to Cassio (II.iii. 256-61) and Othello (III.iii. 155-61) establish it as something both valuable and insubstantial, 'something, nothing'. Othello had of course won Desdemona in the first place through his tales of danger which gave him a reputation for heroic valour, and when he believes she has been false, part of his reaction is a fear of the social dishonour that attends a cuckold:

> But, alas, to make me
> A fixèd figure for the time of scorn
> To point his slow unmoving finger at!
> (IV.ii. 53-5)

The horrible irony of his final crime is that he was able to delude himself into thinking that he did naught in hate, 'but all in honor'. It is as an 'honorable murderer' that he is to be regarded, with all the bitter ambiguity the phrase implies. His suicide is as much an attempt to resurrect the reputation of his honourable, soldierly self, 'he that was Othello', as an expression of final despair. It is worth noting that Thomas Rymer, in his notorious attack upon the play, thought Othello's suicide was the *only* action he performed which was at all in keeping with his supposed manly and martial character. 'We see nothing done by him, nor related concerning him, that comports with the condition of a General, or, indeed, of a Man, unless the killing himself, to avoid a death the Law was about to inflict upon him.'[23]

His last speech, as Helen Gardner has pointed out, is closely related to the public self-justification that was expected from great men before their execution.[24] Like Ralegh's three-quarter hour peroration from the scaffold, it is designed to ensure his 'good name' does not perish with him. It begins by recalling the man who had 'done the state some service' and also stresses his great contrition by mentioning the tears that flowed freely from eyes 'unusèd to the melting mood'. However, as it reaches its climax in suicide, the impression is not purely one of heroic assertion, nor of damnable despair, but of tragic self-division and contradiction.

> And say besides that in Aleppo once,
> Where a malignant and a turbaned Turk
> Beat a Venetian and traduced the state,
> I took by th'throat the circumcisèd dog
> And smote him—thus.
> > *He stabs himself*
> > > (V.ii. 352–6)

The effect of this is to objectify the conflict between the two Othellos. We are reminded of the Christian soldier who honourably destroyed his country's enemies but who, this time, must destroy his own 'worser spirit'. The malignant Turk represents the Othello who consciously rejected love and replaced it by 'black vengeance' and 'tyrannous hate'. It is an honourable act to destroy such a being. In the moment of suicide, as throughout the whole play, the conflict in Othello's soul is symbolised by the greater war between Christian and Turk which provides the play's background. For the Renaissance it was a war with absolute moral significance, a struggle to the death between good and evil, Christianity and Islam. Quite early on in the play, Shakespeare makes a direct link between this wider conflict and the individual's self-betrayal when he causes Othello to exclaim,

> Are we turned Turks, and to ourselves do that
> Which heaven hath forbid the Ottomites?
> > (II.iii. 160–1)

Some years later, Sir Thomas Browne was to seize on the same analogy when he used the great naval battle against the Turks in 1571 to image the contrarieties of his being: 'Let mee be nothing if within the compasse of my selfe, I doe not find the battell of *Lepanto*, passion against reason, reason against faith, faith against the Devill, and my conscience against all.'[25] Othello's outward situation, a Moor at the head of a Christian army in 'a town of war' which is in the front line of this global conflict, is an exact counterpart to his inner state. In destroying the Turk within himself he is able to vindicate his honour as a Christian soldier only by an act epitomising the self-betrayal which made such a vindication necessary. Rather than labelling his suicide 'noble' or 'despairing', we should respond in the manner of Epernon's famous lines from *The Tragedy of Byron*:

> Oh of what contraries consists a man!
> Of what impossible mixtures! Vice and virtue,
> Corruption and eternnesse, at one time,
> And in one subject, let together loose!
> We have not any strength but weakens us,
> No greatness but doth crush us into air.
>   (V.iii. 189–94)

Othello was 'great of heart' and so an honourable suicide was to be expected, Cassio tells us. Yet his highly developed sense of honour was one of the causes of his tragedy, making him an 'honorable murderer' and plunging him into a fatal despair. What Iago says of Cassio could equally be applied to Othello himself:

> do but see his vice.
> 'Tis to his virtue a just equinox,
> The one as long as th'other. 'Tis pity of him.
>   (II.iii. 117–19)

To express such contradictions and their self-destructive consequences, there is no more fitting dramatic image than suicide.

CHAPTER 5

Lucrece Figures

And chastitie a clew, that leads to death.
(Massinger)

The divergent Christian and classical ideas of honour noted in the last chapter found a temporary meeting-ground in the case of women who killed themselves to preserve their chastity. Classical respect for chastity evident in the Greek worship of Artemis and Athene, and in Roman reverence for the vestal virgins, harmonised with early Christianity's obsession with physical purity.

> It [Christianity] regarded purity as the most important of all virtues, and it strained to the utmost all the vast agencies it possessed, to enforce it. In the legislation of the first Christian emperors we find many traces of a fiery zeal. Panders were condemned to have molten lead poured down their throats. In the case of rape, not only the ravisher, but even the injured person, if she consented to the act, was put to death.[1]

Pagan thirst for the glory of a noble suicide found a counterpart in the zeal for martyrdom which gripped the early Church, a zeal of such proportions

> that many were baptized only because they would be burnt, and children taught to vex and provoke the executioners, that they might be thrown into the fire.[2]

It was in this moral climate that the Church honoured Pelagia, Domnina, and Sophronia, all of whom took their own lives rather than suffer rape. Donne gives a lyrical paraphrase of the passage from St Ambrose's *De Virginibus* which describes the deaths of

St Pelagia, her mother, and her sisters:

> And then, having dressed herself as a bride, and going to the
> water, 'here,' says she, 'let us be baptized; this is the baptism
> where sins are forgiven, and where a kingdom is purchased, and
> this is the baptism after which none sins. This water regenerates,
> this makes us virgins, this opens heaven, defends the feeble,
> delivers from death, and makes us martyrs. Only we pray to God
> that this water scatter us not, but reserve us to one funeral.'
> Then entered they as in a dance, hand in hand, where the torrent
> was deepest and most violent.[3]

Such unqualified admiration soon ceased to be orthodox, as
the Church became hostile to all forms of suicide. St Augustine,
in the *City of God*, pays particular attention to the problem of
women who died defending their chastity, and devotes a chapter
to Lucrece herself, as being the most famous example of such a
suicide. Although calling her 'noble', he proves with rigorous
logic (given his premise that suicide is a form of murder) that she
must be at fault. Either she was an adulteress, or she murdered an
innocent. 'If she be an adulteresse, why is shee commended? If she
bee chaste why did shee kill her selfe?' The answer given is that
'being a *Romain*, and covetous of glory, she feared, that if she
lived stil, that which shee had indured by violence, should be
thought to have been suffered with willingnesse';[4] an answer
which deliberately gives her motives unacceptable to a Christian.
St Augustine's discussion may seem a little abstract and external,
with insufficient imaginative sympathy for the psychological
turmoil of a woman in such a situation, yet his remarks on
Lucrece are an important stage in the long-term transition from a
pagan ethic based on social considerations of honour and shame
to a Christian ethic with a more absolute sense of innocence and
guilt. And in challenging the assumption that morally innocent
women must kill themselves to safeguard their reputation, there
is rationality and humanity as well as theological severity.

His arguments precluded any normal defence of a suicidal act,
so, faced with the unpalatable fact that the church had canonised
a number of these women, he was forced to 'retire to that poor
and improbable defense, that it was done by divine instinct'.[5]
When this cannot be invoked, only pity remains. Elizabethan and

Jacobean writers on suicide generally followed Augustine's mixture of pity and condemnation, rather than Ambrose and Jerome's enthusiastic approval of such deaths, though they recognised that the virgin martyrs were the most problematic of all historical suicides:

> And of those which killed themselves to preserve their chastitie, this charitable judgement is to be given, that though the act which they committed, was unlawfull, how so ever the occasion and intention seemed to be: (for we must not doe evill, that good may come thereof) yet God might give them the sight of their sinne before their soule departed, and so they repenting of it, it was not imputed unto them.[6]

The idea of a last-second repentance was a useful tool in combining natural charity (and the approval of the early Church) with theological orthodoxy, and in fact is resorted to by Shakespeare in *The Rape of Lucrece*. After Lucrece has stabbed herself, the poet adds that 'Her contrite sighs unto the clouds bequeathèd/ Her wingèd sprite' (ll.1727–8).[7] In Christian terms, the reference to her contrition is a necessary prerequisite of her eternal bliss. Such a careful 'saving of appearances' by Shakespeare was hardly necessary, for 'in spite of Saint Augustine's onslaught, chastity-suicide was never altogether established as a sin'.[8] Instead, as the humanists began to reconsider the classical past, Lucrece's case was argued over with renewed vigour so that

> by Shakespeare's day, 'a theme for disputation' is precisely what the classical Lucretia's reputation had become, her conduct with Sextus Tarquinius and her decision to take her own life being matters that were sometimes formally debated *pro* and *contra*.[9]

In theory, this ethical and theological uncertainty could have provided the basis for great drama. The clash of mighty opposites evident in the death of Othello could perhaps have been made apparent in the drama's many Lucrece figures. The interplay between the positive and negative elements of such suicides would have gone far towards making them truly tragic. Something of the sort happens in Shakespeare's narrative poem which juggles fascinatingly with Christian and pagan schemes of value to create a heroine who dies nobly by the standards of her own society, but tragically and unnecessarily by different standards which are insinuated into the poem.

In the drama itself, there are hints of a tragic development in the despair and sense of guilt that overtakes those women who fail to avoid being raped. Merione, in Fletcher's *The Queen of Corinth* (1616–c.1618), cries out,

> Let no good thing come near me, virtue flie me;
> You that have honest noble names despise me,
> For I am nothing now but a main pestilence
> Able to poison all. Send those unto me
> That have forgot their names, ruin'd their fortunes,
> Despis'd their honours; those that have been Virgins
> Ravish'd and wrong'd, and yet dare live to tell it.
>
> (II.iii.Cam.VI, p.23)

In another Fletcher play, *Valentinian* (1610–14), Lucina is so overwhelmed with shame that she tells the Emperor, her ravisher,

> I am worse then thou art; thou mayst pray,
> And so recover grace; I am lost for ever.
>
> (III.i. 66–7)

In no other Jacobean play are the different ways of responding to a chastity-suicide so fully exploited. The options open to the ravished Lucina are made the subject of a three-cornered debate between the woman, her husband Maximus, and his friend Aecius. In Roman tradition, Lucina must die in order to secure her reputation, and this is the view her husband takes. If people read that she lived,

> Must they not aske how often she was ravished,
> And make a doubt she lov'd that more then Wedlock?
> Therefore she must not live.
>
> (III.i. 243–5)

Aecius is more inclined to take the Christian view that her chastity, being a spiritual quality, could not have been taken from her by an act of rape and 'Therefore she must live,/ To teach the world such deaths are superstitious' (III.i. 245–6). The other main argument he uses against her suicide has even stronger Christian overtones. By continuing to live, Lucina may 'draw from that wild man a sweet repentance,/ And goodness in his days to come' (III.i. 210–11):

> For who knowes but the sight of you, presenting
> His swolne sins at the full, and your faire vertues,
> May like a fearfull vision fright his follies,
> And once more bend him right again?
>   (III.i. 213–16)

The different viewpoints are bandied back and forth, until Aecius gives way and tells her to 'go find *Elysium*'. Despite its interest, the argument has no real significance beyond itself since it corresponds to no complexities in the character of Lucina. Whatever she decides to do and whatever she might say about herself, she remains a 'type' of virtue. Fletcher is aware that there are different opinions about the necessity of suicide in such a case, aware too of the shame and despair that can underlie an honourable death, but he makes no real attempt to convince us that Lucina is anything but wholly virtuous.

The reason for this is that although Lucrece figures might be a casuistic problem for theologians, they had long been canonised by poets and playwrights. The chastity they die for is more often than not conjugal chastity, fidelity to their husband or betrothed, rather than actual virginity. St Augustine's criticism of Lucrece ('being a *Romain*, and covetous of glory ...') has less force when one realises that it is more her husband's honour that she dies for than her own; there is an altruistic element in such a death which is quite independent of any search for personal glory. Such altruism is sympathetic, even when one rejects the social ethic which required it. Dying for others, these women are virtually indistinguishable from other constant lovers whose faith is stronger than death. Chaucer's praise of Lucrece in *The Legend of Good Women* is in the context of an imagined order from the Queen of Love[10] for a poem about faithful women, and the majority of female honour-suicides in the drama can be seen as variant forms of martyrdom for love. The playwrights inherited unshakeable literary assumptions about the virtue of such a death and showed little desire to challenge these assumptions. All the women in Elizabethan and Jacobean plays who kill or threaten to kill themselves when faced with rape are presented as fundamentally virtuous and their deaths free from doubt or despair. The scene just described in *Valentinian* is the nearest any dramatist gets to suggesting the ambivalence that attended such suicides outside the confines of literature.

Any examination of character and motive in the drama's many scenes of actual or attempted suicide by women to preserve their chastity leaves an impression of depressing uniformity. The degree of pollution incurred by rape might be questioned, but the honesty of the woman involved is always total and the psychology simple. In this respect the playwrights lagged behind even contemporary observation. Montaigne tells an interesting story of a young woman who threw herself from a high window and then tried to cut her throat to avoid a rape. On being prevented (though not before wounding herself severely),

> she voluntarily confessed that the souldier had yet but urged her with importunate requests, suing solicitations, and golden bribes, but she feared he would in the end have obtained his purpose by compulsion: by whose earnest speeches, resolute countenance, and gored blood (a true testimony of her chaste vertue) she might yet appear to be the lively patterne of another Lucrece, yet know I certainly that, both before that time and afterward, she had been enjoyed of others upon easier composition.[11]

Such human inconsistency is entirely absent in the plays under consideration. Indeed, the offer of suicide frequently becomes the definition, rather than merely an illustration, of virtue in a woman. In cases of thin and inadequate characterisation such an offer acts as a kind of ethical shorthand which the audience would have no difficulty in deciphering. The anonymous play *Lust's Dominion* (1600) is populated by a host of cardboard villains whose ambitions and lusts keep the plot moving. The only two virtuous women in the play—Eleazar's wife Maria and Isabella, the Infanta—are easily and conventionally defined as 'good' and singled out from the rest of the cast, by their threats to kill themselves rather than be seduced or raped. Maria, when she learns of Fernando's plan to seduce her, exclaims,

> Then this ensuing night shall give an end
> To all my sorrows, for before foul lust
> Shall soil the fair complexion of my honour,
> This hand shall rob Maria of her life.
>
> (II.iii. 177–80)

When the moment comes, she does not in fact take the poison she has obtained, but gives Fernando a sleeping potion instead. Nevertheless her expression of intent is sufficient to typify her as 'chaste'.[12] Similarly, in a brief dialogue with Eleazar, Isabella proves her honesty by an offer to kill or mutilate herself. Eleazar is forced to pretend that his advances were in jest. This second example is irrelevant to the progress of the plot and is simply there as the most efficient way of defining Isabella as virtuous and her love for Hortenzo as being distinct from the various lusts that have been portrayed.

Altofronto's wife Maria in *The Malcontent* triumphantly passes an equally brief test of her virtue by her husband in his role as Malevole. She reacts to his proffer of Mendoza's love with

> *Maria:*   And long as I can die, I will live chaste.
> *Malevole:*   'Gainst him that can enforce how vain is strife!
> *Maria:*   She that can be enforced has ne'er a knife.
>   *She that through force her limbs with lust enrolls,*
>   *Wants Cleopatra's asps and Portia's coals.*
>
> (V.iii. 28–32)

Her scene with Malevole is only just over 30 lines long, but her readiness to kill herself to avoid dishonour is all that is necessary to convince Altofronto—and the audience—of her worth. Like the testing of Castiza in *The Revenger's Tragedy*, the scene is intended to build a bedrock of virtue in a quagmire of evil. The Jacobean playwrights, like most writers, found it easier to convey the reality of evil than to show 'virtue in her shape how lovely'. When the structure of a play called for an image of virtue, the easiest and most conventional virtue to portray was that of the chaste woman. To take another example, the first sign that the morality of Volpone and his 'heirs' is not universal comes in Celia's outburst when Corvino attempts to pander her to the Fox's lust:

> Sir, kill me, rather: I will take downe poyson,
> Eate burning coales, do any thing—
>
> (III.vii. 94-5)

This could be regarded as a pivotal moment in the play, and in fact Volpone suffers his first reverse when Bonario rescues Celia from his attempted rape.

Scenes in which a woman's virtue is tested by a threat to her chastity are frequent in the 'Beaumont and Fletcher' group but often lack an organic relationship with the plays in which they occur. In *The Knight of Malta* (1616-19) the part of seducer is filled by the celibate hero Miranda who goes through a grotesquely inappropriate routine on two separate occasions. Fletcher and his collaborators seem to have taken an especial delight in constructing variations on this theme (thus in *Cupid's Revenge* the lustful Bacha pretends to be chaste, whilst in *The Maid in the Mill* the pure Florimel feigns wantonness) but they never seriously question the ultimate proof of virtue—the offer of suicide. Throughout *The Humorous Lieutenant* (1619) Celia is subjected to a series of tests by the King, who thinks she is not worthy of his son Demetrius. Her final vindication comes in the conventional manner, after she has been threatened with rape:

> *Antigonus:*   Say I should force ye?
>   I have it in my will.
> *Celia:*   Your will's a poore one;
> And though it be a Kings will, a despised one,
> Weaker then Infants leggs, your will's in swadling
>   clouts:
> A thousand waies my will has found to check ye;
> A thousand doores to scape ye: I dare die sir;
> As suddenly I dare die, as you can offer.
>
> (IV.v. 59-65)

After this, the King abandons his objections to Celia as a daughter-in-law and curtails his attempts on her chastity.

In Marston's *Sophonisba* (1605-6) such tests are more artistically related to the main theme of the play—the idea of keeping one's word even in death. Early on Sophonisba says,

Speach makes us men, and thers no other bond
Twixt man and man, but words.
                                        (II.i.vol.II, p.22)

To submit to rape is to break the bond imposed by the marriage
vows (the play opens on the wedding night of Sophonisba and
Massinissa), thus losing a part of one's humanity and descending
to the level of a beast. The lust-crazed Syphax ('Blouds appetite/
Is *Syphax* God') twice tries to rape Sophonisba but she snatches
out a knife and threatens to 'set my soule on wing'. Massinissa's
confidence in his wife's virtue is grounded on his knowledge that
'she can die'. She in fact survives the attempted rape, only to have
her honour tested in a different but parallel way. Massinissa had
guaranteed her freedom but at the same time pledged loyalty to
Rome. When Scipio orders him to bring Sophonisba to him as a
prisoner, there is only one way in which he can be saved from
breaking his word. In killing herself, Sophonisba becomes both
'free' and 'captive', and protects her husband's honour in the
same way as she had done when confronted by Syphax. As in the
Lucrece story, a woman sacrifices herself so that male honour can
be preserved. In this case, Roman power has played the role of
lustful tyrant in threatening the bond between man and wife.

Most of these chastity-suicides have, in fact, an important
political aspect. The equation of tyranny with rape is frequently
made in the drama as, for instance, in Fletcher and Massinger's
The Double Marriage when Virolet attempts to give a thumbnail
sketch of Ferrand's oppressive rule: 'rapes of Matrons,/ and
Virgins, are too frequent' (I.i.Cam.VI. p.324). Lucrece's fame
undoubtedly rested on the political consequence of her rape and
death—the expulsion of the Tarquins. The foulness of Sextus's
crime causes Lucius Junius Brutus to drop his assumed mask of
folly and lead a revolt. The pitiful spectacle of Lucrece's bleeding
body unites the common people behind Brutus and ensures the
success of the rebellion and the end of the Roman monarchy.
Likewise, the main significance of the very similar legend of
Appius and Virginia was the revolt against the decemvirs and the
re-establishment of consular rule it occasioned. From very early
on, the Lucrece story was being shaped as a political myth of
republicanism and revolution. The earliest major narratives
which survive were written down by men with fresh memories of

the assassination of Caesar, memories which influenced their
handling of the story. Marcus Junius Brutus, Caesar's assassin,
himself utilised the myth by claiming direct descent from the man
who overthrew the Tarquins and, indeed, the political content of
the story has always given it renewed currency during periods of
revolutionary upheaval, such as the early 1790s in France.[13] In the
Renaissance, the sexual and political halves of the story were
easily connected by means of the commonplace body/state
analogy and the often stressed relation between good government
of a kingdom and self-government of the passions. Yet the
monarchic and authoritarian ideology of Elizabethan and
Jacobean England was undoubtedly hostile to the revolutionary
and republican thrust of the legend and it is interesting that both
Shakespeare's poem and Heywood's play on the subject
moderate this aspect. Shakespeare makes Lucrece's psychological
and emotional state the centre of his story, only referring to the
fall of the Tarquins in the last stanza. Heywood's rambling play
does cover all the political background but lessens the republican
implications by making Brutus assume single (not consular) rule
when Tarquin is deposed. After the death of Brutus, Collatine
too assumes single command of the country. By these
modifications, Heywood succeeded in extracting some of the
story's political sting.

Yet even when there is no subversive intent, a political
dimension remains integral to the story, and this is maintained in
other Jacobean plays which feature a suicide for chastity. *The
Second Maiden's Tragedy* (1611), a play which is receiving more
attention the more firmly connected it becomes to Middleton,
opens with the 'new usurping Tyrant' installed at court while the
rightful king Govianus remains present but powerless, like
Philaster. The political-sexual parallel is established when the
Tyrant attempts to seize Govianus's Lady as well as his crown.
When the Lady remains true, the Tyrant compares the two
'kingdoms' and realises he rules the lesser one:

> Sure some dream crowned me.
> If it were possible to be less than nothing,
> I wake the man you seek for. There's the kingdom
> Within yon valley fixed, while I stand here
> Kissing false hopes upon a frozen mountain,

Without the confines. I am he that's banished.
                                        (I.i. 140-5)

He surrounds the Lady's house with soldiers who are about to
break in and take her to him, when she asks Govianus to kill her.
His failure to do so (he swoons at the vital moment) is probably a
manoeuvre on the part of the author to leave him guiltless of
innocent blood and therefore able to assume the throne without
difficulty at the end of the play. Instead, she dies nobly by her own
hand, though even this does not place her beyond reach of the
Tyrant's lust. The episodes in which her corpse is exhumed and
painted express the 'unnaturalness' of tyranny and usurpation
even more graphically than the straightforward attempts at rape
which characterise so many of the theatre's tyrants. More
specifically, the idolatrous worship of the painted corpse may be
intended as a dramatic comment on pro-Catholic tendencies in
the Jacobean court.[14]

'The lamentable Tragedie of chaste MATILDA' which
occupies the latter part of *The Death of Robert, Earl of
Huntingdon*, also implies that moral and political problems are
ultimately the same. King John's lust for Matilda produces civil
war, his repentance after her death leads to peace. Although,
technically, Matilda is murdered by John's agent Will Brand for
her stubborn chastity, her death is virtually indistinguishable
from suicide:

Matilda: Art thou not come to kill me from the king?
Brand: Yes
Matilda: And thou art welcom, even the welcom'st man,
            That ever came unto a woefull maid.
                                        (ll.2574-7)

She proceeds to drink willingly 'a full carouse' to John's health
from the cup of poison with which she is presented. At this point,
as was mentioned in Chapter 2, Brand rushes off and hangs
himself in despair. The two faces of suicide are interestingly
juxtaposed but there is no overlap. Neither Matilda nor Brand are
tragic figures since their deaths demand only the most straightforward response. Their respective nobility and guilt are total.

At the end of the play, the dead Matilda is borne in on a bier by

several nuns, '*one carrying a white pendant*'. Written in gold are
the words '*Amoris, Castatis, & Honoris honos*'. This emblematic
spectacle pierces John with contrition:

> And looke my Lords upon his silent woe:
> His soule is at the doore of death I knowe.
> See how he seekes to suck, if he could drawe,
> Poyson from dead *Matildaes* ashie lips.
>
> (ll.3003–6)

By initiating a moral regeneration, Matilda's death 'saves' John
rather than destroys him as Lucrece's death destroyed the
Tarquins. Political freedom is re-established by the conversion of
the tyrant rather than his destruction.

It will be remembered that Aecius, in Fletcher's *Valentinian*,
had urged Lucina to remain alive in the hope that she might win
the Emperor to repentance. The treatment of the political
consequences of rape and suicide in this play makes an interesting
comparison with the examples discussed above. The possibility
that Lucina's suicide would have the effect of overthrowing the
corrupt Valentinian is regarded as an argument against it, since
this is one of the plays in which Fletcher's supposed royalism is
given free expression:

> the hearts of Princes
> Are like the Temples of the gods; pure incense,
> Untill unhallowed hands defile those offrings,
> Burnes ever there; we must not put 'em out,
> Because the Priests that touch those sweetes are wicked.
>
> (I.iii. 19–23)

Aecius's summing-up of the political side of the argument is that
'Death only eases you; this, the whole Empire' (III.i. 219), a point
of view in total opposition to the strongly republican legends of
Lucrece and Virginia, and even the Christian story of Sophronia
and the Emperor Maxentius. When Lucina *does* kill herself, the
revenge of her husband Maximus is carefully stripped of all the
moral authority that the actions of a Collatine or a Virginius
possessed. On hearing of her determination to die, his reaction is,

'She has made a way for *Maximus* to rise by' (III.i. 351). His first step is to plot the death of the noble Aecius who he knows will block any attempt to assassinate the Emperor. His corruption is completed when he abandons his intention of an expiatory suicide and decides to become Emperor himself. Fletcher's point seems to be that rape does not justify revolution nor an honourable suicide a dishonourable revenge. This attitude was presumably very acceptable to the increasingly autocratic Stuarts. When a young Dutch professor used Tarquin as an example of tyranny in a lecture at Cambridge, Laud had the course of lectures stopped because of their 'republican' tone.[15] Later, under Charles II, Nathaniel Lee's play *Lucius Junius Brutus* was similarly banned by the Lord Chamberlain because of its supposed anti-government implications. Fletcher's handling of a similar narrative was designed to avoid such problems.

The formalised presentation of the dead Matilda which was noted above is an indication of the perspective in which the drama's Lucrece figures should be viewed—that of emblem art rather than dramatic tragedy. There is a static, visual, and ultimately undramatic quality about all these honourable women which stems from the unquestioned virtue of their deaths. It is interesting that the two most successful creators of women characters in this period, Shakespeare and Middleton, both wrote a lengthy narrative poem on Lucrece in their youth, whilst neither went on to write a play on such a subject. The obvious dramatic potential of the story tends to be dissipated by the inevitability of the central character's virtue. Far more enduring are the emblematic qualities of such 'a pitifull and lamentable, but yet an honest kind of death'.[16] Lucrece was a favourite subject for painters in the Renaissance and, in the plays themselves, it is the visual element of a death for chastity which often predominates. The most extreme example of this is Antonio's wife in *The Revenger's Tragedy* who does not even have a walk-on part in the play, but whose self-murdered corpse functions as an emblem of chastity which, together with Castiza's honesty and Gloriana's skull, provides a counterweight to the depravity of the court:

Antonio: I mark'd not this before—
            A prayer-book the pillow to her cheek;
            This was her rich confection, and another

Plac'd in her right hand, with a leaf tuck'd up,
Pointing to these words:
Melius virtute mori, quam per dedecus vivere.
True and effectual it is indeed.

(I.iv. 12–18)

As with Matilda on her bier, the emblem is formally completed by
a moralising motto.[17] It is the pitiful spectacle the bodies of these
women provide that is important to the dramatists, not any tragic
conflict in their hearts and minds. At the end of *Appius and
Virginia*, when Virginius is considering clemency for the wrong-
doers, Icilius fetches the body of Virginia before him so that the
freshly bleeding wounds may cry for vengeance. They are more
eloquent than Virginia as an individualised character had been
during life.

The emblematic use of these suicides was a logical product of
the over-simplified response they elicited. Any sense of defeat or
despair is entirely absent. Every playwright was the willing
prisoner of a useful but, in the end, stifling convention. The
constant use of 'death before dishonour' as a shorthand symbol
for ultimate virtue was helpful to the average dramatist in
constructing a play with an easily recognisable moral shape, but
fatal to any subtlety of characterisation and fatal eventually to any
real sense of drama. However, the many Lucrece figures in
Jacobean plays often have a structural and thematic importance
that transcends the stereotyped nature of their role, even as it
arises from it. Whereas the genius of a Webster could make a
'lusty widow' (in Ferdinand's coarse phrase) the moral centre of
his play, lesser dramatists preferred a more conventionally
virtuous woman, a 'figure cut in alabaster' rather than one of flesh
and blood, to provide the structurally necessary opposition to
chaos and depravity. In the Lucrece paradigm they found what
they were looking for.

Ironically, and despite the more formalised rhetoric employed,
the most 'dramatic' and truly tragic of any of these figures is the
heroine of Shakespeare's narrative poem. Despite being morally
innocent, she cannot rid herself of the conviction that she has
been permanently polluted in some way by the rape. The
coexistence of undoubted moral purity with the sense of an
indelible stain generates a tragic duality which is interestingly

symbolised by the way the blood which flows from her self-inflicted wound divides into two streams.[18]

> Some of her blood still pure and red remained,
> And some looked black, and that false Tarquin stained.
>   (ll.1742-3)

Like Othello, who tries to kill the malignant Turk within him, Lucrece tries to destroy the corrupted part of herself but can only do so by destroying the whole person. The waste which results from such self-division and self-destruction closely anticipates the mature Shakespearean tragic effect.

CHAPTER 6

Deaths for Love

It has been ever my opinion,
That there are none love perfectly indeed,
But those that hang or drowne themselves for love.
(Webster)

Love-suicides are only one aspect of the paradoxical relationship which has frequently been seen to exist between love and death.

> He that examines these matters more closely, will find that the beginning of the *vita amorosa* proceeds from death, because whoever lives for love, first dies to everything else.[1]

The bitter-sweet nature of love was regarded as a direct consequence of its closeness to death:

> And Orpheus also called Love *glukupikron*, that is *dulce amarum*, because love is a voluntary death. As death it is bitter, but being voluntary, it is sweet.[2]

Although ancient philosophy tended to classify love as a 'sickness', and death as one of its violent effects, many classical legends of suicidal lovers were to become hagiographies when the medieval religion of love made its appearance in European life and literature. The myths of Iphis and Anaxarete, Dido and Aeneas, and Pyramus and Thisbe, took on new life. They were supplemented by more historical stories, such as that of Antony and Cleopatra, and the many Roman wives who chose to accompany their husbands in death. The constancy of Cornelia, Portia, Arria, and Paulina[3] showed that love and faith could be stronger than the fear of death.

More surprisingly, a violent passion could be regarded not as transcending death, but as itself a form of death in its annihilation of individuality. This is the sense of the Friar's words to Romeo:

> These violent delights have violent ends
> And in their triumph die, like fire and powder,
> Which, as they kiss, consume.
>
> (II.vi. 9–11)

This intuition is embodied in the frequent Elizabethan and Jacobean use of the word 'die' to refer to the culmination of the sex act, the 'little death'. If Denis de Rougemont's thesis is accepted, the passion of the courtly lover always has death as its ultimate and undeclared aim. The passion which the troubadours celebrated, and which underlies so much of the subsequent literature of love, derives its transfiguring intensity from a continued obstruction and frustration. In one sense, death is the most serious obstruction of all and 'thus the one preferred above all'.[4] In another sense, death means the end of all obstruction and hence the attainment of a union which would be impossible on earth:

> Between joy and its external cause there is invariably some gap and some obstruction—society, sin, virtue, the body, the separate self. Hence arises the ardour of passion. And hence it is that the wish for complete union is indissolubly linked with a wish for death.[5]

Suicide is the most direct expression of that wish, and it is not surprising that the classic pattern of love tragedy should involve suicide by at least one, if not both, of the protagonists. It is convenient to enquire at this point whether such deaths were in any way associated with despair.

An obvious association appears in the tendency of lovers' woes to become coloured by the motifs of religious despair; for the most distinctive feature of courtly love was the continual religious reference of its rhetoric. A classic instance of such rhetoric is the Drayton sonnet which begins 'AN EVILL spirit your beautie haunts Me still':

> Before my Face, it layes downe my Despaires,

And hastes Me on unto a sudden Death;
Now tempting Me, to drowne my Selfe in teares,
And then in sighing to give up my breath;
    Thus am I still provok'd, to every Evill,
    By this good wicked Spirit, sweet Angell Devill.[6]

Such a transference of imagery meant that literature's tragic lovers could be referred to as hanging themselves, the form of suicide most closely associated with despair and never resorted to by Stoic or virgin. The despair which might be emblematised by the rope round a lover's neck was more likely to be a despair of his lady's mercies than of his soul's salvation, but moralists, as distinct from poets, thought the latter was necessarily implied by any offer of suicide. 'Elizabethan theology saw lovers as especially susceptible to the temptations of suicide, but suicide was regarded as being equally damning for them as for others.'[7] Suicide was the ultimate proof of the tortures endured by lovers, even as it was the gateway to eternal torture of a different sort:

> this I say, doth most plainely prove their griping griefes, to be of all other most painefull: seeing that so many of them do willingly runne into the everlasting paines of hell fire, by cruelly murthering them selves, that they may thereby escape and rid them from the broyling brandes of *Cupide*, which will not long indure: being muche like unto *Aesopes* fishe, that foolishly leaped out of the frying pan into the fire.[8]

In the various Elizabethan translations and adaptations of Italian *novelle* there is often a curious wavering between the moralistic and romantic interpretations of love-suicides. Robert Wilmot's play *Tancred and Gismund*[9] is a classic tragedy of courtly love in which the lovers, Guiszard and Gismund, 'move unquestioningly through a quasi-religious ritual which purifies their souls to the point where they can convert the terrors of death into joy.'[10] Murdered by Gismund's father Tancred, Guiszard

> was far more glad apaide
> Death to imbrace thus for his Ladies sake,
> Then life, or all the joyes of life he said.
> (ll.1467–9)

Gismund proves herself faithful to her lover by swallowing poison. As she lies dying, she says,

> Now passe I to the pleasant land of love,
> Where heavenly love immortall flourisheth.
>
> (ll.1725-6)

This is a clear reference to the courtly doctrine that

> joining the loved one in death qualifies the lover as one of Cupid's saints and ensures that the two meet in the 'Paradise in which dwelt the god of love, and in which were reserved places for his disciples'.[11]

Yet before Gismund took the step which would lead to a lovers' paradise, the Chorus had intervened with comments about the shamefulness and damnability of suicide. Gismund brushes these protests aside, but at the end of the play the Epilogue stands over the self-murdered corpses of Gismund and the guilt-stricken Tancred, and proclaims,

> Lo here the sweets of grisly-pale despaire, ...
> With violent hands he that his life doth end,
> His damned soul to endless night doth wend.
>
> (ll.1859-64)

His words are clearly apt enough in Tancred's case, but are heresy in terms of the religion of love which colours so much of the play's thought and action.

Such obvious inconsistency is generally avoided in Jacobean plays but can be detected, I believe, in some of Massinger's work. In *The Maid of Honour* (c. 1621-32), Adorni, despite being in love with Camiola, nobly agrees to try to rescue Bertoldo, the man Camiola wants to marry:

Camiola: you will do this?
Adorni: Faithfully, Madam. But not long live after.
>   [*Aside.*]
>   (III.iii. 208-9)

His aside establishes his credentials as a martyr for love, and confirms his nobility as nothing else could. When the time comes however, he does not kill himself but instead delivers a lengthy and orthodox attack on suicide:

> This Roman resolution of self-murther,
> Will not hold water, at the high Tribunall,
> When it comes to be argu'd; my good Genius
> Prompts me to this consideration. He
> That kills himselfe, to avoid misery, feares it,
> And at the best shewes but a bastard valour;
> This lifes a fort committed to my trust,
> Which I must not yeeld up, till it be forc'd,
> Nor will I: Hee's not valiant that dares dye,
> But he that boldly beares calamitie.
>   (IV.iii. 117–26)

In his handling of tragic love, as in everything else, 'Massinger can never really decide between his conservative ethics and the romantic values of Fletcher.'[12]

It is this indecision which lies behind the painfully contrived ending of Fletcher and Massinger's *The Double Marriage*. The idea seems to have been to stage a love tragedy without making the lovers, Virolet and Juliana, guilty of suicide. Without prior explanation, Virolet suddenly appears disguised as his own worst enemy. The hitherto entirely passive Juliana promptly stabs him, mistaking him for Ronvere. The traditional association of love and death is invoked ('This the new marriage of our souls together'), but when Juliana *'Offers to kill her self'* and complete their 'marriage', she is dissuaded in moralising terms:

> If you do thus, we shall not meet in heaven sweet;
> No guilty blood comes there.
>   (V.i.Cam.VI, p.398)

Instead, she simply sits down beside his body and, after a while, she too is discovered to be 'cold and stiff'. The corpses are 'sad examples of *Ferrands* tyranny' and even sadder examples of the contrivances to which Massinger's orthodoxy drove him.[13]

Renaissance tension between Christian and romantic values, apparent in the creaking plot of *The Double Marriage* and the ending of *Tancred and Gismund*, was more subtly exploited by

Shakespeare in the most famous of all love tragedies, *Romeo and Juliet*.

> What is in the other Elizabethan works drawn from the Italian novelle a crudely mechanical mixture of a glorification of passionate love and a Christian moralistic condemnation of it is in Shakespeare's *Romeo and Juliet* a subtle blend of these two ingredients.[14]

Although it requires a peculiar insensitivity to the tone of the play to regard the lovers as guilty sinners,[15] it is true that the spectre of Despair hovers in the background at various key moments. After the sentence of banishment has been passed, Romeo '*offers to stab himself*' but is prevented by the Nurse and Friar Laurence. The Friar's reaction emphasises the unnatural, bestial quality of suicide:

> Hold thy desperate hand.
> Art thou a man? Thy form cries out thou art;
> Thy tears are womanish, thy wild acts denote
> The unreasonable fury of a beast.
> (III.iii. 108–11)

Juliet also despairs when she learns of Romeo's exile, and there is an implication (which could be brought out in performance) that the very ropes with which Romeo was to have ascended to her bedroom will be her means of suicide:

> He made you for a highway to my bed;
> But I, a maid, die maiden-widowèd.
> Come, cords; come, nurse. I'll to my wedding bed;
> And death, not Romeo, take my maidenhead!
> (III.ii. 134–7)

The words 'despair' and 'desperate' occur several times more before the end of the play and Romeo, if not Juliet, appears to have a sense of guilt. Meeting Paris outside the tomb he exclaims,

> tempt not a desp'rate man....
> Put not another sin upon my head

By urging me to fury.

(V.iii. 59-63)

In his last speech, he sees his soul and body as shipwrecked, but there is no sign that they are cast up on the shores of a 'pleasant land of love'.

> Come, bitter conduct; come, unsavory guide!
> Thou desperate pilot, now at once run on
> The dashing rocks thy seasick weary bark!
> Here's to my love! [*Drinks.*] O true apothecary!
> Thy drugs are quick. Thus with a kiss I die.
>
> (V.iii. 116-20)

The essential innocence of the lovers, and the courtly traditions which underlie the play, mean that their deaths are free from the *guilt* of the despair implied here, but not its bitterness. There is virtually no reference to a future paradise of lovers in which they will be reunited (except perhaps for Juliet's punning description of the poison as a 'restorative'), but only the sense of being consumed together by 'engrossing death'. Their suicides lead them neither to hell nor a lovers' heaven but only to a dark and silent, though shared, tomb. Christian despair and courtly apotheosis were, indeed, two of Shakespeare's 'ingredients', but this antithesis is overshadowed by a persistent and finally total identification of love with death. The words of the Prologue,

> From forth the fatal loins of these two foes
> A pair of star-crossed lovers take their life.

tell us, through the oxymoron 'fatal loins' and the double sense of 'take their life', that Romeo, Juliet, and their love are 'death-marked' from birth. This impression is reinforced by the many images of the bridal bed as the grave and Death as the bridegroom. The suicides are the final link in this chain of images and constitute a fatal marriage, 'the one kind of marriage that Eros was ever able to wish for'.[16] It is the unique single-mindedness with which Shakespeare pursues the theme that love and death are finally indivisible that is one reason why *Romeo and Juliet* stands as the paradigm for all future love tragedies. Suicide is not a gateway to an after-life of any sort, but the most complete expression of love's bitter-sweetness. 'As death it is bitter, but being voluntary it is sweet.' Notoriously resistant to conventional tragic analysis in terms of character and fate or innocence and guilt, *Romeo and Juliet* achieves its power and coherence by relentlessly expressing, like the Tristan and Iseult myth, the dark perception that intense romantic passion cannot be separated from a drive towards death.

No Jacobean love tragedy attempts such a sustained expression of the dual meaning of the word 'die', but it is in the metaphysical contrarieties of desire and death, rather than in a shifting relationship with despair, that the main interest of Jacobean love-suicides is to be found. Such suicides can be divided neatly, if not always certainly, into two categories: the melancholy and despair of betrayed or unrequited lovers, and the fatal marriages of constant lovers who '*Both* Live, *or both together* Dye'.[17]

Suicides in the first category were often discussed by the writers of contemporary medical and psychological treatises, and their occurrence predicted as part of the accepted pathology of love-melancholy. Marriage was frequently recommended as the only certain cure, 'otherwise it is to be feared, that through Madnesse and Impatience, they will make away themselves, either by drowning or hanging'.[18] A striking, although not altogether typical example in the drama is Young Bateman in William Sampson's *The Vow Breaker* (1625–36). His betrothed, Anne Boote, breaks her vows to him and marries another man while he is abroad. On returning, he falls into a suicidal despair and actually hangs himself on stage. Not the least interesting aspect of the play is the way it makes explicit the superstitious fears which prompted the customary desecration of the suicide's corpse:

> *Anne:* My best counsell is that you bury him as the custome of the
>   Country is, and drive a stacke through him; so perhaps I
>   that had no quietnes with him, whilst he liv'd, may sleepe in
>   peace now he's dead.
>
>   (II.iv. 123–6)

Such precautions were apparently not taken, for Young Bateman's vengeful spirit arises to haunt the faithless Anne, until she too is driven to suicide.

The melodramatic details of the haunting, and the horror of the onstage hanging (as in *The Spanish Tragedy*, the dangling body is discovered by the boy's father), place Young Bateman at some remove from such genteel and sophisticated melancholics as Philaster and Aspatia. These latter examples are the product of a different literary tradition (that of prose romance, whereas *The Vow Breaker* was based on a ballad) and illustrate the widely-held belief that love-melancholy tended to afflict the nobler sort of person. This belief was strengthened by a failure to realise that the term frequently used for the disease, 'heroical melancholy', derived from the Greek 'Eros' and had nothing to do with heroes. Suicidal tendencies were a recognised feature of 'heroical melancholy', but it is the sweetness of death rather than the bitterness of despair which is usually conveyed. In Beaumont and Fletcher's *Philaster* (1608–10), the hero and the two women who love him, Arethusa and Eugenia (the latter disguised as the page Bellario), all wander about in a pleasantly pastoral setting, wishing for death. As in *Thierry and Theodoret*, the expression of a noble willingness to die is accompanied by a distinct lift in the quality of the verse:

Philaster:	Oh, but thou doest not know
	What tis to dye.
Bellario:	Yes, I doe know my Lord:
	Tis lesse then to be borne; a lasting sleepe,
	A quiet resting from all jealousie:
	A thing we all persue: I know besides,
	It is but giving over of a game,
	That must be lost.

(III.i. 252–8)

Philaster himself is not to be outdone, and in the course of the play sets some sort of record for offers to commit suicide. The artificiality of his suicidal melancholy is brought out when he runs away on the one occasion when death *really* threatens, giving the explanation

I must shift for life;
Though I doe loathe it. I would find a course,

To lose it, rather by my will then force.
                                    (IV.iv. 102–4)

All the characters in *Philaster* would, one feels, prefer to 'cease upon the midnight with no pain' rather than actually kill themselves, yet if the play had been a tragedy rather than a tragicomedy, the morbid romanticism of the various lovers might well have darkened into madness and suicide. This is what happens in Ford's *The Broken Heart*, where Penthea represents the furthest conceivable tragic development of the 'melancholy lover' type. Her death song, like so much of Ford's earlier play *The Lover's Melancholy*, would have blended perfectly with the atmosphere of *Philaster*:

> Love is dead. Let lovers' eyes,
>   Locked in endless dreams,
>   Th'extremes of all extremes,
> Ope no more; for now Love dies,
>   Now Love dies, implying
> Love's martyrs must be ever, ever dying.
>   (IV.ii. 148–53)

In the case of Penthea, such sweet sorrow transcends the decorative and the pathetic, for it is mingled with the terrible despair and sense of shame that result from her attempts to live by one code of ethics while believing in another. She equates her forced and loveless marriage with rape and, as with Shakespeare's Lucrece, her moral sensibility expresses itself through a strong feeling of actual physical pollution, a pollution which can only be removed by suicide.

> There is no peace left for a ravished wife
> Widowed by lawless marriage. To all memory
> Penthea's, poor Penthea's name is strumpeted.
> But since her blood was seasoned, by the forfeit
> Of noble shame, with mixtures of pollution,
> Her blood—'tis just—be henceforth never heightened
> With taste of sustenance.
>   (IV.ii. 146–52)

In a general way, Penthea's madness owes something to the Ophelia scenes in *Hamlet*. Whether or not one accepts Carroll Camden's view that 'it is more "the pangs of despiz'd love" which cause her tragic fate than the death of Polonius',[19] it is clear that the lovesick maidens of Stuart drama often resemble Ophelia. The lines in *The Broken Heart* which Eliot admired so much,[20]

> Remember
> When we last gathered roses in the garden
> I found my wits, but truly you lost yours.
> (IV.ii. 119–21)

are part of a theatrical tradition, which Shakespeare helped to establish, that the songs and speeches of mad and melancholy lovers should contain floral references. The Jailer's Daughter in Fletcher and Shakespeare's *Two Noble Kinsmen* (1613–16) sings of 'Nothing but willow, willow, willow' and sits making posies of rushes, surrounded by thousands of different-coloured water flowers. Her thoughts of suicide and actual attempt to drown herself make her hopeless passion for Palamon in every way typical of theatrical love melancholy. In her speeches there is a certain tension between her fear of a damning suicide and her desire for the 'natural' lover's death from a broken heart or (in Renaissance medical theory) a broken liver. The hell which awaits suicides ('if one be mad, or hang, or/ Drown themselves, thither they goe,') is contrasted with the paradise which awaits other tragic lovers:

> we Maids
> That have our Livers, perisht, crackt to pieces with
> Love, we shall come there, and do nothing all day long
> But pick Flowers with *Proserpine*.
> (IV.ii.Cam.IX, p.356)

This antithesis, which appears frequently as a kind of footnote to Jacobean explorations of love and death, does little, however, to modify the overall effect of the scenes with the Jailer's Daughter. *In toto*, they convey a cruder version of the pastoral melancholy evident in Gertrude's 'There is a willow grows askant the brook' speech.

Desire for death and a decorative pastoralism are also the two main characteristics of the neglected Aspatia's presentation in *The Maid's Tragedy*:

> the unfrequented woods
> Are her delight, and when she sees a bancke
> Stucke full of flowers, she with a sigh will tell
> Her servants, what a prittie place it were
> To burie lovers in, and make her maides
> Pluck 'em, and strow her over like a corse.
> (I.i. 88–93)

In so far as this transcends its conventionality, it is through a sense of bitter-sweet morbidity akin to that conveyed by the famous emblem of shepherds and skull, entitled *Et in Arcadia ego*. This morbidity becomes more apparent in the conversation Aspatia has with her maids:

> if you needs must love
> (Forc'd by ill fate) take to your maiden bosomes
> Two dead-cold Aspicks, and of them make lovers,
> They cannot flatter nor forsweare; one kisse
> Makes a long peace for all.
> (II.ii. 22–6)

Like most similar characters in the drama, Aspatia is a pathetic rather than a tragic figure, with little room for tragic development. Yet through her interaction with Amintor, the man who broke faith with her in order to marry Evadne, Beaumont and Fletcher are able to achieve a more significant conjunction of love, death, and despair than appears in the conventional conceits of a melancholy maiden.

Amintor is also a melancholy and suicidal figure for much of the play, but his growing sense of guilt makes him somewhat more interesting. Meeting Aspatia while on his way to Evadne's bed, he suffers a momentary pang of conscience but is able to convince himself that this is merely his great sensitivity:

> my guilt is not so great
> As mine owne conscience, too sencible,

Would make me thinke.

> (II.i. 133-5)

It is only the humiliations that he suffers later from Evadne and the King, that bring him to acknowledge his fault:

> The faithlesse sin I made
> To faire *Aspatia*, is not yet reveng'd,
> It followes me.
>
> (III.i. 218-20)

The suicide he contemplates is not a lover's death but an act of despair, prompted by his shameful position as surrogate husband, and a sense of the shameful behaviour which led him to that position:

> I feare my friend that you will loose me shortly,
> And I shall doe a foule act on my selfe
> Through these disgraces.
>
> (III.ii. 181-3)

Aspatia, the woman he wronged, is offstage throughout the middle of the play but in Act V fulfils her desire for death by appearing in disguise and forcing Amintor to a duel. Amintor's comments make it clear that she was seeking suicide, not revenge:

> what dost thou meane,
> Thou canst not fight, the blowes thou makst at me
> Are quite besides, and those I offer at thee
> Thou spreadst thine armes, and takst upon thy brest
> Alas defencelesse.
>
> (V.iii. 101-5)

Before he is able to learn her identity, Evadne enters with a bloody knife, fresh from her murder of the King. When Amintor rejects her advances, she too kills herself. Faced with the dead and the dying, Amintor sinks into the depths of despair:

> This earth of mine doth tremble, and I feele
> A starke affrighted motion in my bloud,

> My soule growes weary of her house, and I
> All over am a trouble to my selfe.
>
> (V.iii. 177–80)

Yet when the dying Aspatia reveals herself to Amintor, 'the miracle occurs which carries his soul beyond despair'.[21] Aspatia's love and forgiveness act as agents of comfort which save Amintor from himself. When she dies, 'Though he despairs of being able to continue life without love's blessing, his love does enable him to transcend his former despair and to die affirming the vision of love which she has granted him.'[22]

Amintor's dying words are conclusive evidence of his redemption. He is now one of love's martyrs who can expect a reunion with the beloved after death:

> The soule is fled for ever, and I wrong
> My selfe, so long to loose her companie.
> Must I talke now? Heres to be with thee love.
>   *Kils himselfe*
>
> (V.iii. 242–4)

By focusing on the redemptive power of love, *The Maid's Tragedy* bridges, within itself, the two major categories of love-suicides noted earlier. The second category, the type of union which Amintor finally attains with Aspatia, is the subject of the remainder of this chapter.

Just as the melancholy of the unrequited lover can be seen as a secular equivalent to the despair of the believer who believes himself excluded from grace, so the fatal marriage of constant lovers has its counterpart in Christian desire to be made one with Christ. For George Strode, one of the cases in which it was lawful for a Christian to desire death was 'for the perfecting and full accomplishment of that conjunction and union which we have in Christ Jesus our head'.[23] It is the mystic's conviction of a union beyond the grave which transfigures so many lovers' deaths in the drama, even as it tends to place them beyond the confines of tragedy. In the early anonymous play *Soliman and Perseda* (1589–92), Fortune, Love, and Death argue, between the Acts, over who should be the Chorus. Death has the strongest case, having destroyed all the main characters, but is not unopposed:

Death:	But I bereft them both of love and life.
Love:	Of life, but not of love; for even in death
	Their soules are knit, though bodyes be disjoyned:
	Thou didst but wound their flesh, their minds are free;
	Their bodies buried, yet they honour me.

(V.v.5-9)

The capacity of true love to transcend death is often set against lust's inability to escape from its bodily prison. The imagery of *The Second Maiden's Tragedy*, as well as the sensational developments of the plot, makes this antithesis a major theme of the play. Before killing herself, the Lady gives eloquent expression to the idea of a union in death:

Govianus:	Must I lose thee then?
Lady:	Th'are but thine enemies that tell thee so.
	His lust may part me from thee, but death, never;
	Thou canst not lose me there, for, dying thine,
	Thou dost enjoy me still. Kings cannot rob thee.

(III.iii. 142-6)

In contrast, the Tyrant's reaction to her suicide shows a conviction that the marriage with death annuls all earthly contracts:

> O, she's destroyed, married to death and silence,
> Which nothing can divorce: ...
> I've lost the comfort of her sight for ever.

(IV.ii. 27-30)

These different attitudes are strikingly symbolised in the events at the end of the play. Govianus, who believed that love would never yield to death, is visited by the Lady's spirit which comforts him with loving looks. The Tyrant develops a necrophilic obsession, and is poisoned while kissing the Lady's painted corpse, an empty shell from which the soul has fled.

Despite the grotesque form his feelings take, the Tyrant's 'I've lost the comfort of her sight for ever' contains a potential for tragedy which is missing in the overwhelming assurance of a lovers' paradise which is so often expressed in the drama. Love-suicides, because they involve neither guilt nor despair, and look forward to a 'pleasant land of love' beyond the grave, are hardly out of place in the worlds of romance and comedy. The anonymous manuscript play *The Fatal Marriage, or a Second Lucretia* describes the fortunes of three pairs of lovers and could, one supposes, be termed a tragicomedy since Galeas and Lucrece kill themselves while the others get married in a more normal way. The speeches leading up to the double suicide are laced with religious imagery and, through the famous name of the heroine, emphasise the honour of the impending deaths.

Lucrece: wee die
                to consecrate a tombe to constancy
                and I that Lucrece wth my latest breath
                utter this *Maxime, true love outlastes death*
Galeas: yet this weele add unto the mouth of ffame
                A Lucrece lov'd and di'de to prove the same.
                            (ll.2200–5)

The fortunate endings of the other plots encourage the view that the suicides were just as valid, and just as happy a form of marriage, as the weddings which follow. 'Nothing is here for tears, nothing to wail/ Or knock the breast', and nor is there in most of the theatre's deaths for love. Such suicides are not tragic expressions of failure and suffering, but act as guarantees of the constancy and strength of passion. 'It is worthy the observing, that there is no passion in the mind of man so weak, but it mates and masters the fear of death,' wrote Bacon,[24] and to be unprepared to die for love was, in literature, a confession that your passion was weak indeed.

One is often aware of a kind of contest between the various characters over who will prove themselves the more noble. When a family feud threatens the marriage of Clarissa and Mentivole in Fletcher's *The Fair Maid of the Inn*, the following scene takes place:

Clarissa: Death's the worst then
                And he shall be my Bridegroom. [*Offers to kill herself.*]
Mentivole: Hold Clarissa, his loving violence needs must
                Offer in spite of honor—

[*He snatches away her knife, and sets it to his own breast, she staies his hand.*]
(V.i.Cam.IX, p.215)

Something similar happens at the end of *Love's Sacrifice* (1632), when the Duke and Fernando 'kill themselves for love of the dead Biancha in what amounts to a contest to join her in heaven'.[25] Ford's play is in many ways an archetypal courtly love tragedy, but fails totally to achieve a tragic effect. In Ford's hands the convention of the shared coffin or tomb takes on the qualities of a macabre bedroom farce when the Duke's last farewell to his murdered wife is interrupted by Fernando rising out of the opened tomb in his winding sheet. After an argument about who belongs beside her, they both kill themselves, Fernando calling 'I come *Biancha*' whereas the Duke, owing to his greater burden of guilt, is only able to 'creepe to thee—to thee—to thee *Bi-an-cha*'. The automatic nobility of the three leading characters (there are several suicide offers prior to the scene at the tomb) is, of itself, untragic, as is the pervasive feeling that there is a place in heaven for love's martyrs. Yet it would be wrong to blame the basic conventions of love tragedy for the defects in Ford's play, for those conventions are manipulated with great success by Shakespeare in *Antony and Cleopatra*.

Facing page 112 of Farnham's *Medieval Heritage of Elizabethan Tragedy* is a late fifteenth-century depiction of the suicides of Antony and Cleopatra. Arieh Sachs gives a vivid description of this picture, which

> uses Antony and Cleopatra to portray a study in criminal despair. Cleopatra's face merely registers this emotion as she holds the serpents to her bare breasts. Antony, however, who energetically pierces himself with a huge sword, is a pure personification of abstract Evil. His face is set in a determined expression of malice. His overgrown black hair gives him an extemely diabolical look.... The picture's message is clear: 'This is the Devil's work,'[26]

Sachs somewhat exaggerates the effect of a rather poor work of art, but there *was* a tradition in which Antony and Cleopatra were regarded as *exempla* of lust and finally, of despair. Not surprisingly, this is the view that Thomas Beard took of Cleopatra, when he included her in a list of famous classical suicides. He concluded,

> Thus the Lord doth infatuate the minds of wicked and ungodlie persons and such as have no true knowledge nor feare of the true God in their hearts, making them instruments of his vengeance, and executioners of his wrath upon themselves.[27]

It was by reading the works of popular moralists like Beard that Franklin M. Dickey was able to arrive at his opinion that

> Instead of seeing Antony and Cleopatra as patterns of nobility and of a deathless love, the Elizabethan reader must have seen them as patterns of lust, of cruelty, of prodigality, of drunkenness, of vanity, and, in the end, of despair.[28]

As Kenneth Muir has pointed out,[29] such a pseudo-historical conclusion ignores the fact that there was more than one traditional way of portraying the lovers. Chaucer included Cleopatra, because of her faithfulness at the last, in *The Legend of Good Women*, and pre-Shakespearean *dramatic* versions of the story emphasise the mixture of nobility and irresponsibility to be found in the protagonists. This mixture is the key to Shakespeare's play, but the suicides of Antony and Cleopatra are not intended to express this kind of moral ambiguity. Although their downfall may have various moral implications, their choice of a self-inflicted death carries little or no suggestion of the guilt and despair which Beard would have seen as an inevitable consequence of their irresponsible lives. Within the context of the play, Cleopatra's question

> then is it sin
> To rush into the secret house of death
> Ere death dare come to us?
> (IV.xv. 83–5)

seems wholly rhetorical. The dominant shaping influence on our response is undoubtedly the literary convention of the fatal marriage, with its emphasis on death as mystic union rather than tragic separation or moral retribution. Like the stories of Pyramus and Thisbe, and Romeo and Juliet, the narrative allows each lover to believe the other dead, making every decision to die a decision to join the beloved in death. Antony's desire to be 'A bridegroom in my death, and run into't/ As to a lover's bed', and Cleopatra's less flamboyantly metaphorical but equally significant reference to Antony as her 'husband' are clear indications that we are witnessing a marriage in death at the end of the play rather than just the final stage in a tragic fall. Moreover, both lovers have the mystical conviction, common in courtly romance, that they are going to a paradise of love beyond the grave, a place 'where souls do couch on flowers', a place which will be the 'new heaven, new earth' required by infinite desire. Yet it would be incorrect to say that simply by following the conventionally positive view of suicide in love tragedy, Shakespeare annihilates all the play's dualities in a transcendent and strictly 'comic' climax. The effect is considerably more complex than that, and relies on more than one of suicide's many significances.

To begin with a relatively marginal point, in the death of Antony (though not of Cleopatra) there is some suggestion of the self-betrayal and self-division symbolised in other Shakespearean suicides, notably that of Othello. As the principal site of the play's thematic conflicts, it is not surprising that Antony, as he falls, should appear to be a man increasingly at war with himself. This is expressed, from the end of Act III onwards, in a flurry of small but cumulatively significant details. He tells his followers,

> My very hairs do mutiny: for the white
> Reprove the brown for rashness, and they them
> For fear and doting.
>
> (III.xi. 13–15)

adding, a few lines later, 'Let that be left/ Which leaves itself.' Enobarbus's acid comment 'When valor preys on reason,/ It eats the sword it fights with' (III.xiii. 199–200) also creates the image of a man in paradoxical conflict with himself, and this is given a more literal expression by Caesar's tactic of placing Antony's revolted followers in the front line of his army 'That Antony may seem to spend his fury/ Upon himself' (IV.vi. 10–11). All this means that when the heroic and Roman notion that 'none but Antony/ Should conquer Antony' is fulfilled through suicide, there may be darker, less heroic implications of self-laceration and civil war within the soul. His heart is not merely pierced by his sword but 'splitted', according to Decretas.

Yet in the final analysis, Antony's suicide seems not so much an image of a man against himself, of a man trying to destroy a part of his being, as the one moment when the different sides of himself—honourable soldier and devoted lover—can converge in a precarious unity. He dies to join Cleopatra in a lovers' paradise, but also to maintain his military honour by avoiding capture. 'Antony succeeds by his death in bringing to complete reconciliation what in his life were constantly and inevitably in conflict, his honor as a Roman and his love for the Egyptian queen.'[30] There is a similar duality of motive and hence a similar merging of the play's thematic contraries in the suicide of Cleopatra. She seeks a marriage in death ('Husband, I come ...') which will mock Roman ambitions, but is also asserting her royal dignity and freedom from capture in a way which is entirely comprehensible within the Roman scheme of values. Although her death is 'after the high Roman fashion', the means chosen (a serpent) is thoroughly Egyptian in its symbolism. The drive towards union characteristic of the fatal marriage convention encompasses not merely the two lovers but the whole range of thematic and imagistic dualities in the play.

In this respect, the suicides are a logical culmination of a process which has been evident throughout, a process in which the various contraries—imperial and amatory, Roman and Egyptian, public and personal, male and female—are continuously seeking to merge and intermingle in the relationship of Antony and Cleopatra. Caesar refers scornfully to Antony as being 'not more manlike/ Than Cleopatra, nor the queen of Ptolemy/ More womanly than he' (I.iv. 5–7), and one of Cleopatra's games was to dress Antony in her clothes whilst she wore his sword Philippan. More generally, throughout the whole play the principal means through which the power of their love is celebrated and heightened is, paradoxically, the imagery of empire—the crowns and crownets. One cannot imagine Antony and Cleopatra giving away all their kingdoms and continuing to live and love as private citizens, since it is the power to give away kingdoms which gives their love its special quality. Although it reaches towards a 'new heaven, new earth', their relationship is also inextricably tied to worldly status and worldly ostentation.

It is a typical amatory gesture of Antony's to make Cleopatra queen of various countries he has conquered, and to do so, moreover, in a particularly public way (III.vi. 1-19). Likewise, the occasion when Cleopatra first captured Antony's heart on the river Cydnus was one of glorious and expensive public display. In a different connection, Caesar speaks of the need for ostentation in love, 'which, left unshown,/ Is often left unloved' (III.vi. 52-3) and this seems to be a key to understanding how the relationship of Antony and Cleopatra achieves 'nobleness'. The power of the line 'I am dying, Egypt, dying' depends on its use of Cleopatra's title rather than her name.

But although their relationship brings together the contraries of love and empire, it does not dissolve them in some magical synthesis. A tension always remains between the sacrifice of identity associated with the drive towards erotic union, and the insistence upon status, self-assertion, and competitive ostentation which characterises this particular erotic relationship. The act of suicide, as mentioned already, seems to be the one moment in which all this can come together—the same deed signifying a sacrifice of the self on love's altar and a glorious assertion of the self through the upholding of personal honour. Although in some sense Antony and Cleopatra die together as tragic lovers, they also die apart, Cleopatra having the last Act to herself in regal isolation. As well as being steps towards an absolute and fatal union in the manner of *Romeo and Juliet*, their suicides have something of the air of an individualistic nobility contest. Antony is anxious not to prove less noble than either his queen or Eros, whilst Cleopatra self-consciously imagines the dead Antony rousing himself to praise her noble act. They seek to triumph over Caesar, but also over each other. In this latter contest, the more premeditated magnificence of her end gives Cleopatra the victory. The famous anticipation of their union beyond death, 'I am again for Cydnus,/ To meet Mark Antony', by recalling that first river meeting, should remind us that Cleopatra's drive towards erotic fulfilment cannot be separated from her love of self-display.

But if suicide does bring together for a moment the contradictory urges of the lovers towards both erotic self-annihilation and worldly self-assertion, and if, through this, it expresses simultaneously the more general dualities of the play, are any of the manifold contradictions actually resolved? The answer is surely only in a formal, aesthetic sense. 'Death cannot resolve the paradoxes of their love, but it can fix them in a final form for all time.'[31] Their suicides are able to balance contrary kinds of positive in a precarious stasis, thanks to the varied implications of suicide even when separated from despair. The thematic fluctuations of the play are stilled for a moment in the deed 'which shackles accidents and bolts up change' (V.ii. 6). As she prepares for suicide, Cleopatra, previously linked with Isis the moon-goddess as a mistress of change, becomes for a moment 'marble-constant', like a statue. The implied simile is highly appropriate, since by giving a formal unity to contradictions which cannot be logically resolved, suicide is functioning here like a work of art, functioning like Shakespeare's own complex art. Once Charmian has adjusted the slipping crown, the paradoxical and pleasing picture of selfless lover and assertive monarch is complete. It cannot last long, of course, but art's triumph is always a precarious one.

CHAPTER 7

Stoicism and Roman Deaths

Do you enquire the road to freedom? You shall find it
in every vein of your body. (Seneca)

In the historical Morality *Apius and Virginia* (1559–67), the
suicide of the corrupt judge Apius is due to the workings of
Justice and Reward who appear in person at the end of the play.
They order Apius to be removed to prison where he promptly
kills himself in despair. His death is reported by Virginius:

> Oh noble Justice duty done, behold I come againe,
> To shew you that Apius he him selfe hath lewdly slaine,
> As soone as he in prison was enclosed out of sight.
> He desperate for bluddy deede, did slea him selfe out right.
> (ll.1148–51)

His suicide functions solely as an image of guilt and retribution
without any heroic or redemptive implications. In this it differs
markedly from the ending of the much later *Appius and Virginia*
by Webster and, possibly, Heywood. At the end of the latter play
(the date of which is uncertain but is definitely seventeenth-
century), Appius and his henchman Clodius are presented with
swords by Virginius, who advises them,

> If you be Romans, and retain their spirits
> Redeem a base life with a noble death.
> (V.ii. 120–1)

Appius follows this advice with a 'resolved constancy', and hopes
that 'this black stain laid on my family' will 'wash with my blood
away'. Clodius, however, continues to beg for mercy and is handed
over to the public hangman. Icilius summarises the significance
of these different reactions:

133

> And note the difference 'twixt a noble strain,
> And one bred from the rabble: both alike
> Dar'd to transgresse, but see their odds in death:
> *Appius* dy'd like a Roman Gentleman,
> And a man both wayes knowing; but this slave
> Is only sensible of vitious living,
> Not apprehensive of a noble death.
>
>   (V.ii. 171–7)

In both plays Appius dies for his sins, but only in the later play is his 'Roman death' distinctively Roman.

A greater historical awareness—or at any rate a greater freedom to express such an awareness—was one of the fruits of the rapid secularisation of the drama. The additional dramatic uses of suicide were a by-product of this. By the Jacobean period, suicide had become one of the ways of defining Roman *mores* and Roman character in the theatre. Maurice Charney thought that a major reason for treating Sheakespeare's Roman plays as a group was their shared and distinctive approach to suicide: 'The foremost defining element for the Roman character in Shakespeare is the willingness to commit suicide rather than live ignobly or suffer death by another hand.'[1] Like the attempts at imitating Roman costume which Henry Peacham's famous *Titus Andronicus* drawing shows, an openly expressed admiration for suicide lent historical conviction to plays with Roman settings.

But if suicide was indeed a way of defining *romanitas*, which of the elements making up the complex Renaissance view of Rome and Roman values were being connoted? Broadly speaking, 'Roman deaths' in the theatre were acts of honour (of a distinctively military, patriotic, and 'manly' kind), acts asserting political freedom, or acts consistent with Stoic philosophy. In the historical deaths of Cato and Brutus all three categories were combined, and they overlap in many of the drama's suicides. A general classical concern with personal honour (seen as a matter both of outward reputation and inner integrity) merges with the heroic individual's resistance to tyranny which in turn merges with Stoic concepts of the autonomy of the rational man. Despite the importance of Stoicism in Renaissance thought, it was probably the assertion of patriotic and soldierly values which had the most positive emotional impact on a theatre audience. In all cases, however, the tendency is towards heroic theatricality rather than the more ambiguous conflicts of tragic drama. Yet the very form of self-assertion involved ('No hand could conquer Cato but his own') carries with it, as always, at least a potential implication of tragic self-betrayal and self-defeat, a potential fulfilled in Shakespeare's treatment of Brutus.

Fletcher's *Valentinian* is one of the best examples of how, in a Roman play, a willingness to commit suicide can be seen as the final proof of virtue, the centrepiece of the play's moral structure. *Valentinian* has many anachronistic Christian overtones but in one respect it is the most Roman play of them all. Five characters kill themselves, and three more think of doing so. The first of the many suicides, that of Lucina, has already been discussed in Chapter 5. Whatever the ramifications of the debate which precedes it, it is clearly a noble act which confirms her purity whilst damning the Emperor who drove her to it. As part of her husband's crooked path to revenge, the loyal Aecius, 'who is indeed the Bull-wark of the Empire', is made the subject of suspicion. Valentinian orders his death and sends an honest captain, Pontius, whom Aecius had cashiered for 'disloyal' remarks, to kill his former commander. Their confrontation is an opportunity for each to vie with the other in appearing the more honourable—a favourite Fletcher situation. Pontius seems about to carry out his orders when, like Eros, he suddenly turns his sword against his own breast, proving conclusively that, all along, he had been 'no traitor'. Aecius's reaction goes beyond the straightforward praise of valour one might expect:

> Is there an houre of goodnesse beyond this?
> Or any man would out-live such a dying?
> Would Cesar double all my honours on me,
> And stick me ore with favours, like a Mistris;
> Yet would I grow to this man: I have loved,
> But never doated on a face till now:
> O death thou art more than beautie, and thy pleasure
> Beyond posterity:
>
> (IV.iv. 227–34)

A similar 'doting' takes place in *Bonduca* after Petillius has seen Bonduca's daughters kill themselves. Both cases are typical of

Fletcher's constant efforts to give a slightly perverted refinement to even the most conventional of stage emotions.[2]

Aecius's own suicide follows almost immediately, and his last speech is perhaps the most forthright praise of a Roman death to be found in the drama:

> hold my good sword,
> Thou hast been kept from bloud too long: Ile kiss thee,
> For thou art more then friend now, my preserver:
> Shew me the way to happinesse, I seeke it...
> Now for a stroak shall turne me to a Star:
> I come ye blessed spirits, make me room
> To live for ever in *Elizium*.
>
> (IV.iv. 251–64)

Aecius had told the dying Pontius that his suicide proved 'thou art a Roman', and his own death offers the same proof. Despite the near perversity of the comradely 'doting', the suicides function as part of a general contrast in the play between traditional manly, military values, felt to be truly Roman, and the effeminate sensuality of the Emperor's court (no doubt with some contemporary application intended). By their self-inflicted blows Aecius and Pontius confirm their masculine and soldierly virtues and become the true representatives of their country, supplanting the lascivious Valentinian.

Even where the minor characters are concerned, suicide continues to act as the ultimate moral dividing line. Phidias and Aretus, the 'bold and faithful Eunuchs' who finally assassinate Valentinian, purge the guilt of revenge with their own deaths. They make a very theatrical entrance, 'Phidias *with his dagger in him*, and Aretus *poysond*'. In deliberate contrast to this, the harrowing scene of Valentinian's death is given an almost farcical conclusion in the discussion of the various panders and flatterers over how to save themselves:

Lycinius:	Let's make our best use, we have mony *Proculus*, And if that cannot save us, we have swords.
Proculus:	Yes, but we dare not dye.
Lycinius:	I had forgot that.

(V.ii. 148–50)

The final twist to the plot also relies on the assumption that suicide either confirms true nobility, or atones for past sins. Maximus acknowledges his guilt and prepares to absolve himself in the Roman manner, but his change of mind places him beyond the pale of audience sympathy and marks the final stage of his corruption:

> For though my justice were as white as truth,
> My way was crooked to it, that condemnes me:
> And now *Aecius*, and my honored Lady,
> That were preparers to my rest and quiet,
> The lines to lead me to *Elizium*;
> You that but stept before me, on assurance
> I would not leave your freindship unrewarded;
> First smile upon the sacrifice I have sent ye,
> Then see me coming boldly: stay, I am foolish,
> Somewhat too suddaine to mine own destruction,
>   ... my deare freinds pardon me,
> I am not fit to dye yet if not *Caesar*.
> (V.iii. 15–31)

His suicide at this point would have been a 'way to make all even' rather than a descent into despair. Instead, the ambition which was cloaked by the justice of his cause leads him away from suicide but towards destruction and damnation. A play like *Valentinian* operates by neatly reversing the Christian ethical implications of every choice the characters make concerning suicide. The one character, Valentinian, who suffers the torments of despair, in fact struggles for life with an energy equal to that shown by his heroic opponents in their search for death.

As with the Lucrece figures, the moral significance of suicide in a Roman play brings with it a political aspect. To show that life or death depend on an exercise of the individual will is to show, however paradoxically and self-defeatingly, that the power of the state is not absolute. The self-inflicted dagger thrusts become blows for freedom and an indictment of tyranny. In the anonymous *Nero* (printed 1624), the author, by simply following his Roman sources, is able to balance the noble suicides of Piso, Seneca, and Petronius against the cowardice shown by the Emperor in his last moments. Petronius's final words are 'Nero, my end shall mock thy tyranny', and the deaths of the various conspirators all assert the fundamental freedom of the noble mind. Nero, however, remains 'cabined, cribbed, confined' by the fear of death and eventually only kills himself to avoid a more painful end. An onlooker's comment, 'So base an end all just commiseration/ Doth take away', tells us that Roman deaths in their fullest sense are achieved only by free men, not tyrants.

In Jonson's *Sejanus* suicide becomes a major symbol of the older, republican virtues which have withered away in the Rome of Tiberius. Arruntius, in effect the play's commentator, makes an indignant and eloquent retort to the claim that times have changed:

> Times? the men,
> The men are not the same: 'tis we are base,
> Poore, and degenerate from th'exalted streine
> Of our great fathers. Where is now the soule
> Of god-like CATO? he, that durst be good,
> When CAESAR durst be evill; and had power,
> As not to live his slave, to dye his master.
> (I. 86–92)

The other republican heroes Arruntius refers to are Brutus and Cassius, also suicides.[3] He ends by saying,

> There's nothing *Romane* in us; nothing good,
> Gallant, or great: 'Tis true, that CORDUS say's
> *Brave* CASSIUS *was the last of all that race.*
> (I. 102–4)

In Act III the implications of this speech are fulfilled in symbolic action. When Silius is accused before the Senate, Jonson departs slightly from his sources for both dramatic and emblematic effect:

> The words of Tacitus at least lead us to suppose that the suicide of Silius took place elsewhere than in the open court; that is, than on the stage. Jonson in the teeth of Horace chose to make it happen there, to the immense advantage of the whole scene which issues in this tragic climax.[4]

By his death Silius is able to show literally that Roman blood runs in his veins and that, '*Brave* CASSIUS' was not '*the last of all that race*'. In this context, *romanitas* is identified with republicanism, whereas in another instance it might be typified by martial prowess. In both cases, the underlying concept is patriotism—something which all Renaissance commentators admired in the Romans. In what is perhaps the bleakest of all Jacobean tragedies, the death of Silius is the only moment in which the audience can feel emotionally positive about anything.

> The coward and the valiant man must fall,
> Only the cause, and manner how, discernes them:
> Which then are gladdest, when they cost us dearest.
> *Romanes*, if any be here in this Senate,
> Would know to mock TIBERIUS tyrannie,
> Looke upon SILIUS, and so learne to die.
>> (III. 336–9)

The different reactions to his suicide ('O, desperate act!' 'An honorable hand!') do not point to a genuine ambivalence as they might in a non-Roman play, but simply represent the different political standpoints of the onlookers. As with most Roman deaths, the suicide of Silius has more significance as a political act than as an individual tragedy. One responds to the heroic outward gesture, but not to an inner conflict of the soul. In this sense, the drama's many Roman heroes, considered in artistic rather than ethical terms,

> differ not from those colossic statues,
> Which with heroic forms without o'erspread,
> Within are nought but mortar, flint, and lead.
>> (*Bussy D'Ambois*, I.i. 15–17)

The tendency to harden into a heroic posture was strongly encouraged by Roman Stoicism, and it is the relation of suicide and despair in the drama to Stoic attitudes, whether in a Roman or contemporary setting, which will occupy the remainder of this chapter.

As a philosophy which placed more emphasis on the inward adherence to absolute rational values than on considerations of outward show and public honour, Stoicism might be thought to have had less obvious theatrical potential than the more social and patriotic ethic which shaped so much of Roman life. But chief among the many passions which the Stoic sought to master was the fear of death, and in overcoming *that* fear (a victory most directly demonstrated by a calmly chosen suicide) there were many opportunities for striking heroic and theatrical poses. 'The contempt of death is the true and lively source of all noble and commendable actions,' wrote the Renaissance neo-Stoic Guillaume Du Vair,[5] and it was this aspect of Stoicism which proved most useful to the Elizabethan and Jacobean playwrights, whose tragic heroes frequently crown their passionate lives with gestures of Stoic fortitude in the face of death ('We cease to grieve, cease to be Fortune's slaves,/ Nay cease to die by dying'). The great influence is of course Seneca, with his rhetorically ostentatious obsession with death and suicide, rather than the original Greek Stoics. 'The ethic of Seneca,' declared T.S. Eliot unsympathetically, 'is a matter of postures. The posture which gives the greatest opportunity for effect, hence for the Senecan morality, is the posture of dying.'[6] Eliot suggests that the theatricality of Senecan Stoicism is ultimately hollow. Certainly Stoicism of any kind, whatever local theatrical effects it might generate, is an uncertain basis for tragic drama since, paradoxically, the more the hero conforms to Stoic principles, the less tragic he becomes. If no evil *can* befall the good man how can he participate in a tragedy?

> The logical aim of Stoic doctrine is complete resignation in man so far as the active life is concerned. In tragedy the only struggle which a Stoic hero could consistently make would be the effort to know that evil did not exist, that he ought to remain calm because his misfortunes were in no sense true misfortunes—in short, that the tragedy in which he was participating was no true tragedy at all.[7]

The suicide which a Stoic hero might commit would not be an act of despair in any sense of the word, but a calm and rational choice devoid of guilt or fear. It would be the final and conclusive proof that misery had no way of reaching him, since the thousand doors of death each offered an escape from it. The ultimately untragic nature of such a suicide is conclusively demonstrated in two plays of Chapman, the one professional dramatist who could be said to hold definite Stoic beliefs as opposed to simply borrowing Stoic attitudes for dramatic purposes.

Chapman's first and most successful tragedy, *Bussy D'Ambois* (c.1604), showed the destruction of a proud and passionate aspirer, one who 'like a thunderbolt/ Look'd to have stuck and shook the firmament'. Its sequel, *The Revenge of Bussy D'Ambois* (c.1610), is a sequel in more than one sense, for Clermont not only revenges his brother's murder but, in his own character, corrects the passionate faults which destroyed Bussy. The later play 'is the most complete and whole-hearted of a number of attempts by previous dramatists to show us the Stoic Wise Man in a world of Neronian equivocation.'[8] 'This absolute Clermont', this 'Senecal man' is moved neither by grief nor joy but preserves a calm reasonableness throughout the play.

> Chance what can chance me, well or ill is equal
> In my acceptance, since I joy in neither,
> But go with sway of all the world together.
> (III.iv. 159–61)

Whereas the tragic hero might rail against 'the false huswife Fortune', the Stoic hero receives 'Fortune's buffets and rewards' with 'equal thanks'. The idea of conforming to the sway of the world is repeated several times by Clermont in sententious but not ineffective verse:

> God hath the whole world perfect made and free,
> His parts to th'use of th'All; men then that [be]
> Parts of that All, must, as the general sway
> Of that importeth, willingly obey
> In everything without their power to change.
> (III.iv. 58–62)

Such a philosophical solution to the problem of evil brought in its wake insoluble dramatic problems. Clermont's passivity is fundamentally undramatic and is peculiarly ill-suited to the role of blood-revenger which is thrust upon him. The Stoic paralysis of emotion which grips the play continues till the end. When the revenge is finally accomplished through an honourable duel,

Chapman proceeds to unsheath the last weapon in the Stoic's armoury—suicide. Superficially it would be possible to regard Clermont's death as part of the traditional workings of the revenge plot. However just the revenge, blood must be repaid with blood and the hero's suicide, as in *The Spanish Tragedy*, could provide this conventional expiation. Chapman deliberately excludes this element from Clermont's death, however, and the explicit motive is the death of Clermont's friend, the Guise:

> None favouring goodness, none but he respecting
> Piety or manhood—shall I here survive,
> Not cast me after him into the sea,
> Rather than here live, ready every hour
> To feed thieves, beasts, and be the slave of power?
> I come, my Lord! Clermont, thy creature, comes.
> *He kills himself*
> (V.v. 188-93)

Whatever audience sympathy might have existed for suicide on account of a 'friendship chaste and masculine', was surely dissipated from the start by Chapman's casting of the Guise as Clermont's noble friend. The one fact which every Englishman would remember about the Guise was his implication in the St Bartholomew's Day Massacre. The manner in which this objection is brushed aside in the course of the play seems almost calculated to alienate a Protestant audience:

Clermont: The Massacre? I thought 'twas some such blemish…
             Had faith and true [i.e. the Catholic] religion been
                                                     preferr'd,
             Religious Guise had never massacred.
                                          (II.ii. 205-34)

In the absence of a respectable motive, Clermont's suicide begins to appear faintly ridiculous. Its main function is probably to indicate that for the Stoic Wise Man, 'the door is always open'. However comforting such a thought may be, it does not produce a tragic conclusion. Indeed, the failure of all Chapman's plays, apart from *Bussy D'Ambois*, to achieve the stature of great tragedy 'is in great measure due to the fact that Stoicism negates the premises from which such tragedy develops.'[9]

If Clermont D'Ambois has all the appearance of a figure specially constructed to epitomise a philosophical viewpoint, Chapman's other Stoic hero Cato, in *The Tragedy of Caesar and Pompey* (1605–13), came ready-made, so to speak. Cato's austere integrity, his incorruptible pursuit of a life according to reason and justice, and his great patriotism, were all freely acknowledged during his lifetime, even by his political opponents. Having sided with Pompey against Caesar as the best way to try and preserve the Republic, he committed suicide at Utica after the defeat of Pompey at Pharsalia. After his death he became a legend, an exemplary figure for both Christian and pagan writers: 'This man was truly a patterne, whom nature chose to shew how farre humane vertue may reach, and mans constancie attaine unto.'[10] Yet the manner of his death meant that, from Augustine onwards, he was also a figure of controversy, the undoubted merit of his life only exacerbating the arguments over his death.[11] As an apparently virtuous and honourable suicide, he became a site for conflict within the imperfect Renaissance synthesis of Christian and pagan values. Rather than accepting his suicide as a Stoic victory over the passions, some Christian writers felt driven to attack it as the consequence of giving way to passion:

> The Holy Spirit judges not of valour by the same measures as profane men, who extol Cato to the skies for committing suicide lest he should fall into the power and hands of Caesar: for he either feared, or could not bear to see him, or sought to catch renown by an act of such prodigious horror. Thus he was crushed and extinguished either by despair, or grief, or some other perturbation of mind; any of which motives are foreign from true fortitude.[12]

Such unhistorical distortions, though they might have made for a more interesting play, are absent from Chapman's portrait. He does not throw doubt upon Cato's motivations, does not show him as tragically overwhelmed by despair or 'some other perturbation of mind', but instead allows him lengthy Stoic arguments proving the total correctness and rationality of his chosen death:

Cato: All just men
            Not only may enlarge their lives, but must,
            From all rule tyrannous, or live unjust.

Athenodorus: By death must they enlarge their lives?
Cato: By death.

(IV.v. 57–60)

Since one cannot live reasonably and justly ('according to nature')
under tyranny, it is better to die than to live unjustly. The just
man's decision to die cannot be challenged because, in Stoic
belief, 'every just man [is] to himself/ The perfect'st law' (IV.v.
71–2). The emphasis on reasoned argument in the closing scenes
robs the play of a good deal of possible emotional impact.
Moreover, there is no real doubt that Chapman largely endorses
Cato's position, since the epigraph for the play, 'Only a just man
is a free man', is derived from Cato's arguments in favour of
suicide. Stage arguments which are felt to come directly from the
author usually have a weakening effect on a play and *Caesar and
Pompey* has never had many admirers, yet it is a much less
schematic play than is commonly believed, and its climactic
suicide, although hardly tragic, embodies much of the play's
moral complexity.

   To begin with, what is one to make of the bizarre 'comic' scene
(II.i) in which Fronto, 'a ruined knave' who has the symbolic red
beard of Judas, tries to hang himself but is prevented by a devil-
figure called Ophioneus? Does this not deliberately complicate
the play's Stoic premises by introducing a Christian image of
suicide as despair which will project a shadow over the final scenes
of the play? Possibly, but I think one can argue that the ultimate
effect of this scene is to support rather than question Cato's
decision to die. In the sort of world which seems to be emerging
from the collapse of the Republic, a world fit only for villains, the
devil's temptation ironically is not to kill oneself, as in the
Morality plays, but to carry on living.

Ophioneus: Hold, rascal, hang thyself in these days? The only time
                        that ever was for a rascal to live in!
Fronto: How chance I cannot live then?
Ophioneus: Either th'art not rascal nor villain enough; or else thou
                        dost not pretend honesty and piety enough to disguise
                        it.

(II.i. 25–30)

In such a world, the just man *cannot* live.

Yet there are other ways in which Cato's death does perhaps become problematic in this play. I have said that Chapman does not question his hero's motives, does not deny that Cato's suicide was undertaken as a reasoned act; yet all reasoning proceeds from certain premises and Cato's central premise, that Caesar is a tyrant, is not fully upheld by the play. Although the first Act appears to confirm Caesar as a ruthless and ambitious politician, much of his later behaviour—such as his freeing of the captured Vibius or his regret that Roman blood has been shed—conveys a different impression. Like Shakespeare, Chapman has painted a deliberately enigmatic portrait of 'the foremost man of all this world', with the consequence of rendering questionable all actions predicated upon his 'tyranny'. Cato is in fact preceded in his suicidal decision by the two consuls who (by Chapman's invention) kill themselves on the battlefield of Pharsalia. According to Caesar, they were only too ready to 'forge a tyrant merely in their fears/ To justify their slaughters' (IV.iv. 6–7). He characterises their deaths as 'desperate', and points out that Brutus, whom everyone knows to be noble and patriotic, has been happy to come over to his side.

> Lov'd they their country better than her Brutus?
> Or knew what fitted noblesse and a Roman
> With freer souls than Brutus?
>
> (IV.iv. 35–7)

The questions are entirely rhetorical. They cannot have done, and hence their suicides were unnecessary, unpatriotic, and 'with no Roman spirit'. In view of later history, there are obviously further ironies involved in this citing of Brutus, but in conjunction with the total picture of Caesar in the play, this episode helps to qualify in advance any impression that Cato's death was an absolutely rational act.

> Even if we judge Cato favourably, and assume that he kills himself not in despair or shame, but in the pursuit of a consistent philosophy, Chapman may still be warning us that the rule of reason is as vulnerable in its way as Pompey's impressionability: without knowing all the facts, it is impossible to make a rational decision.[13]

In other words, Chapman is making the same epistemological critique of reason as a basis for action that Shakespeare makes so powerfully in *Julius Caesar* and *Hamlet*. Rather than being the tyrant Cato thinks he is, Caesar perhaps embodies a kind of greatness complementary to Cato's own. The two men could be described in the way that Chapman describes the essential difference between his two Homeric translations:

> In one, Predominant Perturbation; in the other, over-ruling Wisedome; in one, the Bodies' fervour and fashion of outward Fortitude to all possible height of Heroicall Action; in the other, the Mind's inward, constant and unconquerd Empire, unbroken, unalterd with any most insolent and tyrannous infliction.[14]

It is interesting that Caesar justifies his ambition with the same sort of teleological argument about Nature working in all things to an end that Cato uses to prove the immortality of the soul and the resurrection of the body. Both men have a heroic self-sufficiency which is shown as superior to Fortune, and both are contrasted with the weak Pompey, who tries to be first a Caesar and then a Cato, but fails miserably in both endeavours. The play, then, overcomes some of the dramatic problems associated with the Stoic hero by setting him against a different kind of hero in a way which creates its own dramatic tension and which allows us interestingly to question the premises of his 'rational' suicide. But the absence of any passionate sense of failure or any other 'perturbation of mind' in Cato renders the play ineffective as a tragedy. Neither we nor Cato feel enough in the closing scenes. A brief contrast of the suicides of Cato and Clermont with the death of Chapman's earlier hero, Bussy, provides an excellent illustration of the general point I am making in this chapter.

The speeches of the dying Bussy are by no means devoid of Stoic and 'Roman' elements as the following lines, which would not sound out of place in the mouth of Clermont or Cato, amply demonstrate:

> Prop me, true sword, as thou hast ever done:
> The equal thought I bear of life and death,
> Shall make me faint on no side; I am up
> Here like a Roman statue; I will stand

> Till death hath made me marble.
>
> (V.iii. 141–5)

In their context, however, these lines are more thrilling, more tragic, than they could ever be in either of the later plays, for they coexist with the crushing despair and consciousness of failure expressed in:

> let my death
> Define life nothing but a Courtier's breath.
>
> (V.iii. 131–2)

The complexity of response demanded by Bussy's death is made brilliantly apparent in the famous lines, adapted from *Hercules Oetaeus*, about how his fame will wing its way round the world. The passage concludes:

> fly where men feel
> The burning axletree, and those that suffer
> Beneath the chariot of the Snowy Bear;
> And tell them all that D'Ambois now is hasting
> To the eternal dwellers; that a thunder
> Of all their sighs together (for their frailties
> Beheld in me) may quit my worthless fall
> With a fit volley for my funeral.
>
> (V.iii. 151–8)

The heroic Herculean connotations of the Senecan borrowings are juxtaposed with Bussy's realisation that he is the sum of all human frailties, and that his fall is 'worthless'. It is this passionate despair which makes his heroic posture fully dramatic and not merely spectacular. The man who 'reels and falls' at the end of Chapman's greatest tragedy is a 'full creature' and a 'complete man', not a passionless cipher or hollow statue like Clermont, whose suicide, divorced from despair, faithfully reflects the dramatic poverty of Chapman's conception of him.

Marston's Antonio plays are in some ways artistically inferior to Chapman's two Stoic tragedies, but Marston shows a far sounder grasp of the dramatic possibilities of Stoicism in his refusal to accept it at its own valuation: 'His vision of life ... was

one which stressed the incapacity of any single attitude to sustain
itself against the bitter ironies of incessant betrayal.'[15] The major
theme of both *Antonio and Mellida* (c.1599) and its sequel
Antonio's Revenge (c.1600), is the manner in which Stoic control
is constantly undermined by the passions, especially those of grief
and despair. The first speech of the earlier play establishes the
mood of suicidal despair which Stoic resolution will be needed to
counter:

> Heart, wilt not break? And thou, abhorred life,
> Wilt thou still breathe in my enraged blood?
> Veins, sinews, arteries, why crack ye not,
> Burst and divuls'd with anguish of my grief?
> Can man by no means creep out of himself
> And leave the slough of viperous grief behind?
>
> (I.i. 1–6)

Within 30 lines, Antonio has decided to 'make a firm stand',
however. This jerkily presented, though very human,
inconsistency runs through the whole play, and Antonio's
shifting states of mind are paralleled by those of his father,
Andrugio. On his first appearance in Act III, he calls to the earth
to split and swallow his soul, which is 'sunk with grief'. Within a
few lines, he too is able to summon up a Stoic defiance and
'combat with despair and mighty grief':

> There's nothing left
> Unto Andrugio, but Andrugio;
> And that nor mischief, force, distress, nor hell can take.
> Fortune my fortunes, not my mind shall shake.
>
> (III.i. 59–62)

Later on in the play both Antonio and his father sink back into
despair and neither is able to avoid becoming 'vile passion's slave';
but the happy ending postpones any final consideration of the
sufficiency of the Stoic ethic until the more brutal circumstances
of *Antonio's Revenge* force an answer.

This play opens with Andrugio and Feliche, the Stoic ideal of
Antonio and Mellida, both murdered by the tyrannous Piero.
Antonio is naturally plunged into a fresh despair:

> Confusion to all comfort! I defy it.
> Comfort's a parasite, a flatt'ring Jack,
> And melts resolved despair.
> (I.v. 48–50)

Feliche's father Pandulpho, however, takes over the role of Stoic Wise Man left vacant by his son, and refuses to give way to grief:

> Wouldst have me cry, run raving up and down
> For my son's loss? ...
> The gripe of chance is weak to wring a tear
> From him that knows what fortitude should bear.
> (I.v. 76–86)

As in the earlier play, the alternation of despair and resolution continues to be a part of what G.K. Hunter has called the 'figure in the carpet',[16] the underlying pattern which gives coherence to the apparently disorganised action. For instance, the real significance of Antonio's disguise as a fool in Act IV is that fools were commonly linked with Stoics as being the only two kinds of men beyond the reach of passion. But of course Antonio's folly is only an assumed mask. It does not save him from despair and nor, the play suggests, can the mask of Stoic resolution. At one point, Antonio enters with a copy of Seneca's *De Providentia* and after reading its exhortations to endure bravely, makes the valid point that the author wasn't suffering when he wrote it.[17] The inadequacy of Stoicism is finally and dramatically demonstrated at Feliche's funeral, when Pandulpho gives way to emotion:

> I spake more than a god,
> Yet am less than a man,
> I am the miserablest soul that breathes.
> (IV.v. 51-3)

His great line, 'Man will break out, despite philosophy' (IV.v. 46), is the best summary of Marston's intentions in the Antonio plays and represents the only possible tragic perspective in which the Stoic hero can be viewed. The value of Marston's approach is perhaps obscured by the continuing controversy over the nature of his dramatic achievement in general; but he was not the only playwright to find this solution to the dramatic problems posed by Stoicism:

> Shakespeare seems to have realized from the start that the dispassionate and coldly rational figure of the stoic, withdrawn from the arena of human emotions and sympathies, is not a subject for tragic treatment.... The infinitely subtle and penetrating study of Brutus is Shakespeare's comment on the full stoic doctrine of self-sufficiency. He is well aware that 'man will break out despite Philosophy', that there is no convenient philosophical armour easily to be assumed, and proof against these 'Despairs and mighty Griefs', which inhabit the tragic scene.[18]

The suicide of Brutus has a tragic complexity which, unlike most Roman deaths in the drama, defies any straightforward response. The soldierly and Stoic elements are there but in interesting contradiction not harmony, and mixed also with different suggestions, suggestions of failure and punishment. The aspect which I shall consider first is more evident, because more crudely depicted, in the University play *Caesar's Revenge* (acted at Trinity College, Oxford, sometime during the 1590s). The conspirators are quite clearly driven to despair and suicide by Caesar's Ghost, which announces after their deaths,

> Hell take their hearts, that this ill deed have done
> And vengeance follow till they be overcome:
> Nor live t'applaud the justice of this deed.
> Murther by her owne guilty hand doth bleed.
>   (ll.2526–9)

In this play, the retributive aspect swamps all else. In Shakespeare's tragedy it is a relatively minor part of the dramatic function of the suicides, but it should not be ignored. The last words of Cassius are,

> Caesar, thou art revenged
> Even with the sword that killed thee.
>   (V.iii. 45–6)

and when Brutus comes across the bodies of Cassius and Titinius he exclaims,

> O Julius Caesar, thou art mighty yet!
> Thy spirit walks abroad and turns our swords
> In our own proper entrails.
>
> (V.iii. 96–7)

In this context it is interesting to note the reply of the Ghost when Brutus questions its nature. It says it is 'Thy evil spirit, Brutus' (IV.iii. 282), with the implication that, as in the academic play, it will be responsible for bringing him to despair.

Balancing this is the more obvious idea that the suicides of Brutus, Cassius, and Titinius uphold Roman principles of honour which have been articulated throughout the play. In his first conversation with Cassius, Brutus says he loves 'the name of honor more than I fear death' (I.ii. 89), and, after Caesar's murder, he tells the crowd that 'as I slew my best lover for the good of Rome, I have the same dagger for myself when it shall please my country to need my death' (III.ii. 43–6). The last quotation emphasises the patriotic dimension but the concept of honour involved is as much a matter of *personal* autonomy, an assertion of individual freedom from tyranny and the indignities of capture. When Cassius is told by Casca that the Senate mean to make Caesar king, he responds:

> I know where I will wear this dagger then;
> Cassius from bondage will deliver Cassius.
> Therein, ye gods, you make the weak most strong;
> Therein, ye gods, you tyrants do defeat.
>
> (I.iii. 88–92)

This kind of motive fuses easily with Stoic concepts of individual self-sufficiency to produce a comprehensively Roman manner of death, allowing Brutus to address the dead Cassius as 'the last of all the Romans' and Titinius to describe his suicide as 'a Roman's part'. Yet in the case of Brutus particularly, the final impression is not of absolute adherence to a closely linked set of distinctively Roman values. Instead, the impression is one of human inconsistency and self-contradiction.

The crucial passage is the conversation Brutus has with Cassius at the beginning of Act V, concerning the consequences of defeat:

Cassius:	What are you then determinèd to do?
Brutus:	Even by the rule of that philosophy
	By which I did blame Cato for the death
	Which he did give himself—I know not how,
	But I do find it cowardly and vile,
	For fear of what might fall, so to prevent
	The time of life—arming myself with patience
	To stay the providence of some high powers
	That govern us below.
Cassius:	Then, if we lose this battle,
	You are contented to be led in triumph
	Thorough the streets of Rome.
Brutus:	No, Cassius, no. Think not, thou noble Roman,
	That ever Brutus will go bound to Rome.
	He bears too great a mind.

$$\text{(V.i. 99–112)}$$

From this it appears that personal honour and philosophical principles are in direct contradiction, rather than being mutually supportive as they were with Chapman's Cato.[19] Throughout the play Brutus has been presented as a self-divided character ('poor Brutus, with himself at war'), and this image is maintained in his death. A question which naturally arises from the quoted passage is, what exactly is the 'philosophy' which Brutus is unable to adhere to in his hour of crisis? It has been usual to consider Brutus as Shakespeare's portrait of a Stoic. Indeed, according to Marvin Vawter, it is possible that Shakespeare thought of the historical Brutus 'not merely as a Stoic but as one of its chief authorities on the self-sufficiency of virtue-reason, in other words, as a Stoic Wise Man'.[20] Yet, as a fully-fledged Stoic, he would presumably have sanctioned suicide, not found it 'cowardly and vile', and in fact according to Plutarch 'above all the rest he loved Plato's sect best'.[21] The problem is more apparent than real since the philosophy of the historical Brutus, like that of many of his contemporaries, was probably an amalgamation of several Greek traditions incorporating a loosely Stoic emphasis on self-sufficiency and self-control. (Cato was the man 'whom Brutus studied most to follow of all the other Romans'.)[22] Shakespeare, familiar with Renaissance neo-Stoicism which carried the ideals of patience and endurance to their logical conclusion by rejecting suicide, would have had no difficulty in thinking of Brutus as a

Stoic despite his principled opposition to a self-inflicted death.

The highly dramatic about-turn over suicide takes its place as one of a series of contrasts in the play between theory and practice, ideals and actuality, public postures and private feelings. The prime location of these dichotomies is the murder of Caesar itself but many of them also directly relate to the contradictions and inadequacies of Stoic philosophy. To be a Stoic is not to live 'according to nature' but, as in Marston, to adopt an unnatural role which cannot be consistently maintained. Portia, the daughter of Cato, is able to demonstrate that she has inherited the Stoic virtue of constancy by an act of self-wounding. Yet her suicide, when it comes, is not a rational act but the result of being overwhelmed by grief and impatience. Her death leads Brutus to confess privately to his friend Cassius that he is 'sick of many griefs', but in public he puts on again the mask of Stoic equanimity:

> Why, farewell, Portia. We must die, Messala.
> With meditating that she must die once,
> I have the patience to endure it now.
> (IV.iii. 190–2)[23]

Earlier, Brutus had told the conspirators not to show their true feelings,

> But bear it as our Roman actors do,
> With untired spirits and formal constancy.
> (II.i. 226–7)

The discussion of suicide with Cassius is one of the moments when the Stoic act breaks down and deeper feelings emerge to shape events. Or perhaps it would be more accurate to say that one role is displaced by another—the role of Stoic philosopher by that of honourable soldier. The references to himself in the third person ('He bears too great a mind') are a rhetorical indication that Brutus is still maintaining a public persona (cf. 'This is a Roman's part'). The idea that 'Brutus' is a role to be lived up to is reinforced by the odd episode during the battle in which Lucilius goes round impersonating Brutus. When the deception is uncovered, Lucilius says that, alive or dead, the real man 'will be found like Brutus, like himself' (V.iv. 25). But the point is that there is no final authentic and harmonious personality, only the continued sense of a man at war with himself.

The tragic hero's assertion of self is often seen as an important constituent of the tragic effect, and it can be argued that this assertion is often made most forcibly through suicide. In choosing their own deaths, Shakespeare's suicides

> are choosing the *manner* of their death, the style. They are declaring that their death shall be an extension of their life, rather than its negation, that death is not an uncharacteristic accident but a final assertion of the power to give personal shape to life.[24]

This is true as far as it goes, but the playwright as well as the character is shaping the significance of a self-inflicted death and, in the case of Brutus, is shaping it to be part of a consistent pattern of self-contradiction and self-division. Hence the latent irony of Strato's admiring tribute,

> For Brutus only overcame himself,
> And no man else hath honor by his death.
> (V.v. 56–7)

Furthermore, as well as signifying a divided will, the suicide of Brutus carries overtones of dejection, weariness, and tragic error unusual in a Roman death. The way in which Cassius is driven to kill himself by not seeing clearly what happened to Titinius ('Alas, thou hast misconstrued everything!' (V.iii. 84)) casts a symbolic shadow of misjudgement over the whole course of the conspiracy, including the death of Brutus which is to follow shortly. Indeed, in his dying words, Brutus is still both deceived and self-deceived:

> My heart doth joy that yet in all my life
> I found no man but he was true to me.
> (V.v. 34–5)

The error into which Cassius fell is described as the consequence of melancholy and Brutus, like Cassius, gives strong evidence of world-weariness and dejection as well as Roman fortitude. Faced with the total failure of all his hopes, he un-Stoically gives way to tears,

> Now is that noble vessel full of grief,
> That it runs over even at his eyes.
> (V.v. 13–14)

and among his last words are expressions of despairing resignation as well as heroic self-assertion:

> Night hangs upon mine eyes; my bones would rest,
> That have but laboured to attain this hour.
> (V.v. 41–2)

Unlike the other suicides in this chapter, the death of Brutus has been carefully made to imply not simply nobility, but despairing failure—the failure of a man divided against himself. That is why he appears the most tragic Roman of them all.

CHAPTER 8

Concluding Remarks

The preceding chapters have indicated, I hope, the immense usefulness of suicide as a dramatic convention during the Jacobean period. Although it has been my concern to demonstrate that a stage suicide only becomes fully tragic when there is a balancing of opposed implications, when dignity grapples with despair, the most common use of suicide in the drama was as an unambiguous label for some particular 'character'. As well as being one of the many 'acts of death' by which the stage was cleared at the conclusion of a tragedy, it was capable of epitomising a wide range of 'types' from 'The tender Conscienc't Despairer' to 'Lovers' and 'Great Spirits'.[1] Used in this way suicide often assumed a major structural and thematic role, even as it relinquished its more tragic possibilities. Indeed, it became the definitive theatrical image for female virtue, passionate love, or the honour of 'an antique Roman'.

The confident manner in which playwrights built scenes, or even whole plays, round these different connotations presupposes an audience capable of responding positively as well as negatively to a suicide in the theatre. Although it is impossible to find a single clergyman prepared to question the damnability of suicide, there were many areas in which Christianity was in conflict with classically-derived values or with 'popular' morality. Renaissance attitudes towards duelling, war, and revenge were as contradictory as they were towards suicide. Whie condemning duelling as un-Christian, Andrew Willet was able to say that 'a man's life ought to be dearer unto him, then his honour or fame',[2] a statement which is in flat contradiction to the precepts of humanist moral philosophy. In a section on suicide in *The Anatomy of Melancholy*, Burton noted, with deliberate irony, that

In wars, for a man to run rashly upon imminent danger, and

156

present death, is accounted valour and magnanimity, to be the cause of his own, and many a thousand's ruin besides, to commit wilful murder in a manner, of himself and others, is a glorious thing, and he shall be crowned for it.[3]

The dramatic value of revenge, as I mentioned in my discussion of *Hamlet*, rested to a large extent on its moral ambiguity, causing Fredson Bowers to conclude his examination of the topic by observing that 'the audience at the theatres seems to have made the customary compromise between a formal set of religious and moral ethics and an informal set of native convictions.'[4] A further, and particularly striking instance of conflict between official and popular moral attitudes has already been referred to in the notes to Chapter 1. To the common people, men who chose to save their goods from forfeiture by refusing to plead and being pressed to death appeared admirably brave, but to moralists such a 'desperate' end was to be condemned.[5]

In considering how an audience might respond more favourably to suicide than the official morality and laws of the age would suggest, it is not enough just to draw attention to the competing philosophies of the Renaissance. There is also the more basic fact of ordinary human sympathy. There are a number of examples during this period of the savage legal penalties against suicide being evaded or mitigated because neighbours, or even officials, pitied the surviving family and sought to prevent the confiscation of the dead man's property. In one case the jury was bribed by the man's brother not to bring in a verdict of suicide. They agreed to the deception because there were so many children and women dependent on the threatened estate. In other cases, neighbours would carry off the property of a suicide before the Crown could get hold of it, or insist that the goods belonged to them as a result of outstanding debts.[6] None of this proves that ordinary people believed in a person's right to commit suicide, but it does show that they were capable of more charity than the law of the land, particularly when the penalties fell upon the living.

The sympathy shown in these examples is evidence for a less moralistic audience than is presupposed in some readings of Renaissance drama, but to look at actual cases of suicide during the period is to be made forcibly aware of the differences between life and art. Although disappointed love and religious anxiety are two motives which appear in both literature and actuality, the general impression one gets from the records of coroners' inquests, ecclesiastical courts, and Star Chamber suits is of commonplace miseries such as illness, bereavement, or debt, untransmuted by the power of art. In 1590, a woman from Feering in Essex appeared before the Church courts on a charge of 'committing fornication with Enoch Greve, who drowned himself, being so burned [i.e. with venereal disease] that he could not abide the pains'.[7] In 1614, Robert Negus testified that Elizabeth Goare, a very poor woman, 'a little before her death, being unmarried, was delivered of a bastard girl and thereupon as this defendant verily believeth, drowned herself'.[8] A still more vivid picture of suicidal suffering is given by John Chamberlain who, after passing a column of pressed soldiers on their way to Dover, wrote,

> Such a rabble of raw and poor rascalls have not lightly [often] ben seene, and go so unwillingly that they must rather be driven then led. You may guesse how base we have growne when one that was prest hung himself for feare or curst hart, another ran into the Thames, and ... drowned himself, another cut of[f] all his fingers of one hand, and another put out his owne eyes with salt.[9]

Such cases seem to have little in common with the death of a Brutus or a Cleopatra, but the real relation of theatrical suicides to life lay not in the private miseries of ordinary people but in the noble public deaths which characterised the age. Whether through actually watching great men mount the tragic scaffold, or through studying the narratives and illustrative woodcuts of heroic self-sacrifice in Foxe's *Acts and Monuments*, the citizens of London had constantly impressed upon them highly theatrical images of greatness of spirit in the face of death. Ralegh, well hated by many in the crowd, proceeded, like a character in a Webster play, to win them over by his courage at the last. 'His death was by him managed with so high and religious a resolution, as if a Roman had acted a Christian, or rather a Christian a Roman.'[10] If, as the words 'managed' and 'acted' suggest, there was something self-consciously theatrical about such an end, so, conversely, the crowds at the theatres must have felt that the dramatists were indeed holding the mirror up to nature when they filled their plays with deaths and suicides of this kind.

As the last quotation points towards ('as if a Roman had acted a Christian, or rather a Christian a Roman'), there was another way in which the theatre's suicides could be said to reflect reality. At a deeper level, they reflected the contradictions of Renaissance culture, contradictions which were often consciously embraced as part of deliberate habits of thinking: 'the tendency to resolve experience into contrariety is so widespread that it may be seen as one of the primary intellectual modalities of the period.'[11] As an act in which the differences between Christian and classical teaching were most sharply felt, and an act in which self-assertion could be achieved only through self-destruction, suicide was supremely fitted to epitomise the contrarieties of the age. In Rosalie Colie's book on Renaissance traditions of paradox, *Paradoxia Epidemica*, suicide is appropriately the final paradox of all. When the many different implications of suicide were combined in a single dramatic character, when failure merged with triumph and guilt with nobility, then the manifestation of a divided Renaissance became the image of human nature itself, conceived of as in a perpetual state of tragic self-division. As part of his argument for the 'radical' nature of Jacobean tragedy, Jonathan Dollimore has recently claimed that the dislocations and contradictions in the presentation of character we find in these plays are a means of subverting Christian humanism by subverting the idea of a unitary subject expressive of a fixed human 'essence'.[12] Yet that 'essence' was most commonly thought of as the meeting-point between polarities, the troubled frontier between opposing forces. Its 'essence' lay in continued contradiction. Such an image was traditional rather than incipiently materialist, but, as a dynamic model of human nature, remains powerfully dramatic even when the world-view it was part of has passed into history. It is an image which suicide, through its own contradictory nature, is especially suited to conveying.

Notes

The following abbreviations are used throughout in the Notes:

Burton: Robert Burton, *The Anatomy of Melancholy.*
Donne: John Donne, *Biathanatos.*
Fedden: Henry Fedden, *Suicide: A Social and Historical Study.*
Lecky: William Lecky, *History of European Morals.*
Montaigne: *The Essayes of Michael Lord of Montaigne,* trans. John Florio.
Sprott: S.E. Sprott, *The English Debate on Suicide from Donne to Hume.*

The full details of these and all other works cited are given in the Bibliography.

CHAPTER 1

1. Sig. B^r.
2. Curtis Watson, *Shakespeare and the Renaissance Concept of Honor,* p.40.
3. Montaigne, IIiii, 'A Custome of the Ile of Cea'; Charron, *Of Wisdome,* IIxi. *Biathanatos,* although written in 1608 and circulated in MS form, was not published till 1647, sixteen years after Donne's death.
4. Nevertheless, an early lexicographer wrote that suicide was 'a word which I had rather should be derived from *sus,* a sow, than from the pronoun *sui,* unless there be some mystery in it; as if it were a swinish part for a man to kill himself' (Edward Phillips, *The New World of English Words* (1658), quoted in Fedden, p.29).
5. A phrase used by Sir John Harington in a marginal note to *Orlando Furioso,* and quoted by Arieh Sachs in 'Religious Despair in Medieval Literature and Art', p.234.
6. *Poems,* ed. Emrys Jones, p.29.
7. See Paul D. Green, 'Doors to the House of Death: The Treatment of Suicide in Sidney's *Arcadia*'.
8. Susan Snyder, 'The Left Hand of God: Despair in Medieval and Renaissance Tradition', p.18.
9. Ibid.
10. Helen Gardner, *Religion and Literature,* p.24.
11. Robert Grudin, *Mighty Opposites: Shakespeare and Renaissance Contrariety,* p.2. See also A.P. Rossiter, *Angel with Horns,* and N. Rabkin, *Shakespeare and the Common Understanding.*

12. As well as Grudin, see Joel Altman, *The Tudor Play of Mind*; Rosalie Colie, *Paradoxia Epidemica: The Renaissance Tradition of Paradox*; and T. McAlindon, *English Renaissance Tragedy*.
13. *The Origins of English Tragedy*, pp.87–8.
14. Donne, p.141.
15. It had been seen in this way by the early Fathers, Tertullian and Origen. In a short essay on *Biathanatos*, Jorge Luis Borges claims that Donne's 'underlying aim is to indicate that Christ committed suicide' ('*The Biathanatos*' in *Other Inquisitions*, p.92).
16. See G. Wither, *A Collection of Emblems, Ancient and Moderne*, IIIxx, p.154. In the foreground of the picture is the pelican gnawing its breast; in the background is the crucifixion. The head-couplet reads:
    > Our Pelican, *by bleeding, thus,*
    > *Fulfill'd the Law, and cured Us.*
17. See Paul D. Green, 'Suicide, Martyrdom and Thomas More'.
18. Chaucer, 'The Parson's Tale', *Complete Works*, p.700.
19. Gordon Rupp, *The Righteousness of God*, p.282.
20. Tyndale, 'Prologue Upon the Epistle of St Paul to the Romans', *Doctrinal Treatises*, p.505.
21. William Willymat, *Physicke to Cure the Most Dangerous Disease of Desperation*, p.3.
22. II Corinthians 7.10.
23. *Shakespeare's Tragic Heroes: Slaves of Passion*, pp.248–9.
24. Una Ellis-Fermor, *The Jacobean Drama*, p.1.
25. p.102. While Shakespeare was embarking on his major sequence of tragedies, the Admiral's Men are known to have performed a play, now lost, on the subject of Judas.
26. Montaigne, Ixviii, p.27.
27. Thomas Tuke, *A Discourse of Death*, p.26.
28. Rupert Brooke, *John Webster and the Elizabethan Drama*, p.101.
29. Montaigne, Ixviii, p.26.
30. Stephen Greenblatt, *Sir Walter Ralegh: The Renaissance Man and His Roles*, p.15.
31. John Sym, *Life's Preservative against Self-Killing*, p.170.
32. Chapman, *The Tragedy of Charles Duke of Byron*, V.iii. 193–4.
33. Burton, Part.1, Sec.1, Mem.1, Subs.1, p.85.
34. *Phaedo*, ed. David Gallop, 61c, p.5. The notes to this edition contain a very full discussion of the whole passage.
35. A. Alvarez, *The Savage God*, p.52.
36. Donne, p.83.
37. *Nicomachean Ethics*, Vxvi.
38. J.M. Rist, *Stoic Philosophy*, pp.241–2.
39. Seneca, *Ad Lucilium Epistulae Morales*, trans. R.M. Gummere, vol.II, Ep.lxx, p.65.
40. Lecky, I, 222.
41. *Ad Lucilium*, vol.I, Ep.xxiv, p.175.
42. *Life's Preservative against Self-Killing*, p.552.
43. Fedden, p.17.

44. Ibid., p.111.
45. 'On Suicide', in *Journal of the History of Ideas* (1978).
46. Fedden, p.39.
47. Ibid., p.116.
48. *Of the Citie of God*, Iix, p.33.
49. See *Summa Theologiae*, vol.XXXVIII, 2a2ae.64, 5.
50. See Alvarez, *The Savage God*, p.61.
51. A study of Bedfordshire coroners' inquests in various years between 1265 and 1317 produced a maximum estimate of only six suicides per million living per annum (*pMa*), compared with the figure of 40*pMa* obtained from a similar study of Nottinghamshire inquests for the years 1530–58. See P.E.H. Hair, 'A Note on the Incidence of Tudor Suicide', pp.36–43.
52. 'The Inner Side of Wisdom: Suicide in Early Modern England', p.566. The casebooks of Richard Napier, an astrological physician, which cover the years 1597–1645 and an area including Bedfordshire, Buckinghamshire, and Northamptonshire, record the names of 11 of his clients who killed themselves, 57 who attempted to, and 99 who wanted to do so. MacDonald points out that none of these names appears among the 262 cases of suicide listed in the coroners' records for those counties in those years. Terence R. Murphy of American University is in the process of completing a much larger survey of all the documentary evidence relating to suicides in England between 1500 and 1700. When this is published it is expected to confirm the hypothesis that there was a very considerable rise in the number of suicides during the mid-sixteenth century.
53. Lecky, II, 56.
54. Curtis Watson, *Shakespeare and the Renaissance Concept of Honor*, p.344.
55. Montaigne, IIiii, pp.174, 175.
56. In the lengthy and useful Introduction to their edition, Michael Rudick and M. Pabst Battin summarise all previous views of *Biathanatos* as well as giving their own detailed and lucid analysis. By comparison, Ernest W. Sullivan's Introduction to his more recent old-spelling edition is considerably briefer and less illuminating, and shows no awareness of Rudick and Battin's arguments.
57. Donne, p.160.
58. Ibid., p.181.
59. The Introduction to the Rudick and Battin edition, p.lxxx.
60. Donne, pp.39–40.
61. *John Donne: Life, Mind and Art.*
62. Sprott, p.25.
63. Ibid.
64. M.D. Faber, in a frequently cited article entitled 'Shakespeare's Suicides: Some Historic, Dramatic and Psychological Reflections', considerably exaggerates the degree of approval for suicide that can be found in works of moral philosophy during this period. The only quotation from a Renaissance moralist he gives which explicitly and

unambiguously praises suicide comes from Lodovick Bryskett, *A Discourse of Civill Life*. According to Faber, Bryskett says that 'it is the part of a stout heart, for a man to kill himselfe rather then to suffer shame or servitude' (Faber, p.34). In fact, this is not Bryskett's opinion at all. It is mentioned by one of the speakers in a fictional dialogue as being 'the judgement of the ancient Romanes', and the context of the remark is a discussion in which suicide is strongly condemned. See Rowland Wymer, 'Lodovick Bryskett and Renaissance Attitudes to Suicide'.

65. *The Golden Grove*, Bk.I, 3rd Plant, xiv, sig. E^r.
66. p.244.
67. John Case, *Speculum quaestionum moralium*, quoted in Sprott, p.8.
68. Agnes Latham, 'Sir Walter Ralegh's Farewell Letter to his Wife in 1603: A Question of Authenticity', p.40.
69. Ibid, p.54. This quotation is from records that the physician Wilson (a government spy) made of his conversations with Ralegh.
70. Stephen Greenblatt, *Sir Walter Ralegh*, pp.114–15.
71. The extant MS is a transcript dated 1679. One objection to its authenticity centred on a reference to a hitherto unknown daughter. The discovery some years ago of Ralegh's 1597 Will, which mentions an illegitimate daughter, has helped to confirm the genuine nature of the letter. See Robert Lacey, *Sir Walter Ralegh*, p.290.
72. Montaigne, IIiii, p.180.
73. Donne, p.47.
74. *Of the Citie of God*, Ixvi, p.27.
75. Burton, 3, 4, 2, 6, p.731.
76. Caesarius of Heisterbach gives some classic examples in *The Dialogue on Miracles*, vol.I, Bk.IVxl ff.
77. '*Doctor Faustus*: A Case of Conscience', p.237.
78. Arieh Sachs gives several examples in 'Religious Despair in Medieval Literature and Art'.
79. Susan Snyder, 'The Left Hand of God', p.56.
80. I, 375.
81. In Skelton's *Magnificence* they are borne by Mischief who follows at the heels of Despair.
82. William Willymat, *Physicke to Cure the Most Dangerous Disease of Desperation*, p.2.
83. Burton, 3, 4, 2, 2, p.713.
84. Sprott, p.13.
85. Although Shepherd's edition leaves the last part of the play (in which this speech occurs) without an Act number, the title page divides the play into five Acts. It should also perhaps be noted that the last two lines quoted have the incorrect speech prefix *Pel.* for *Tel* [lamon].
86. *The Jacobean Drama*, p.223.
87. In Nashe's *The Unfortunate Traveller*, Cutwolfe's fearful revenge on Esdras of Granado concludes with the latter being forced to utter the most appalling blasphemies before being shot in the throat to prevent him repenting of them and avoiding damnation. See *Works*, II, 325–6.

88. *The Pattern of Tragicomedy in Beaumont and Fletcher*, p.42.
89. Harold Jenkins, Introduction to the Arden *Hamlet*, p.144.
90. 'The Case of Hamlet's Conscience'.
91. The Arden *Hamlet*, p.492.
92. 'The Case of Hamlet's Conscience', p.136 n.
93. Examples from outside the drama include Sidney's *Arcadia*, where the Helots achieve military success against the Lacedaemonians by 'grounding their resolution upon despair' (p.94); Browne's *Religio Medici*, where Catholics who determinedly resist religious reform are referred to as 'those desperate Resolutions' (I, 3, in *Works*, I, 12); and Wither's *Abuses Stript and Whipt*, where men who save their goods from forfeiture by refusing to plead and allowing themselves to be pressed to death are said by the common people to show 'a manly Resolution' but, Wither goes on to say, 'sure there is no wise-man wil commend/ Him that so desperately seeks his end' (Sig.H7ᵛ). Not all these examples refer strictly to religious despair, but there is the usual overlap of meaning between the different senses of the word.
94. This point is made by Helen Gardner in *The Business of Criticism*, p.49.
95. The Arden *Hamlet*, p.154.
96. Donne, p.105.

CHAPTER 2

1. *Life of Sir Philip Sidney*, ed. Nowell Smith, p.221.
2. 'The Monk's Tale', ll.559–60, *Complete Works*, p.539.
3. Quoted by Willard Farnham, in *The Medieval Heritage of Elizabethan Tragedy*, p.287.
4. Thomas Newton in his Preface to *Seneca His Tenne Tragedies*, I, 5.
5. R. Smythe, *Straunge, Lamentable, and Tragicall Hystories*, quoted by J.M.R. Margeson, in *The Origins of English Tragedy*, p.136.
6. From the Dedication of *The Revenge of Bussy D'Ambois*.
7. Sig. F3ᵛ.
8. Dominic Baker-Smith, 'Religion and John Webster', in *John Webster*, ed. Brian Morris, p.215.
9. 'Hesiodus correcteth the saying of Plato, that punishment doth commonly succeed the guilt, and follow sinne at hand: for, he affirmeth, that it rather is borne at the instant and together with sinne it self, and they were as twinnes borne at one birth together' (Montaigne, IIv, 'Of Conscience', p.182).
10. *The Philosophie, Commonlie Called, the Morals*, trans. Philemon Holland, pp.545–6.
11. Trans. E. Grimeston, p.373.
12. Farnham, *op.cit.*, p.421.
13. Donne, pp.46–7.
14. Thomas Beard, *The Theatre of Gods Judgements*, IIxii, p.308.

15. 'And he cast down the pieces of silver in the temple, and departed, and went and hanged himself' (Matthew 27.5). 'Now this man purchased a field with the reward of iniquity; and falling headlong, he burst asunder in the midst, and all his bowels gushed out' (Acts 1.18).

16. 'The Function of Imagery in Webster', p.719.

17. Montaigne, IIv, p.182.

18. *The Theatre of Gods Judgements*, Ixxiii, p.150. Compare Andrew Willet's comment on the appropriateness of Saul's death: 'Herein Gods justice appeareth, that as Sauls sword was turned against the innocent Priests, in putting them to death, and against David whom he unjustly persecuted, so now he himselfe should fall upon the edge thereof' (*An Harmonie upon the First Booke of Samuel*, xxi, q.3, p.173).

19. For instance,

> The hell of life that hangs upon the Crowne,
> The daily cares, the nightly dreames,
> The wretched crewes, the treason of the foe,
> And horror of my bloody practise past,
> Strikes such a terror to my wounded conscience,
> That sleepe I, wake I, or whatsoever I do,
> Meethinkes their ghoasts comes gaping for revenge,
> Whom I have slaine in reaching for a Crowne.
>
> (ll.1874–81)

20. Burton, 3, 4, 2, 3, p.719. Theodoric supposedly saw Symmachus's face threatening him in a fish's head. The experience threw him into a grievous sickness from which he died.

21. D.C. Gunby, '*The Duchess of Malfi*: A Theological Approach', in *John Webster*, ed. Brian Morris, p.197.

22. Fletcher (with others), *The Bloody Brother*, II.i.Cam.IV, p.260.

23. So, of course, does Ophelia, but the main consideration in her case is the difficulty of staging her elaborately pastoral drowning.

24. Fredson T. Bowers, *Elizabethan Revenge Tragedy*, p.206.

25. *The Jacobean Drama*, p.152.

26. *Some Versions of Pastoral*, p.48.

27. R.B. Parker, 'Middleton's Experiments with Comedy and Judgement', in *Jacobean Theatre*, ed. J.R. Brown and B. Harris, p.191.

28. M.C. Bradbrook, *Themes and Conventions of Elizabethan Tragedy*, p.234.

29. By Lily B. Campbell, in *Shakespeare's Tragic Heroes: Slaves of Passion*.

30. Calvin, quoted in R.M. Frye, *Shakespeare and Christian Doctrine*, p.152.

31. *The Works of Thomas Nashe*, I, 345.

32. William Perkins, *A Discourse of Conscience*, quoted in Lily B. Campbell, '*Doctor Faustus*: A Case of Conscience', p.224.

33. Webster, *The Devil's Law Case*, II.iii. 154.

CHAPTER 3

1. The Council of Arles (fifth century) pronounced suicide to be the effect of diabolic inspiration.
2. Robert Potter, *The English Morality Play*, pp.47–8.
3. While confessing his sins, Avarice falls into despair but is prevented from hanging himself by Repentance who reminds him of God's mercy. See Passus V, ll. 279–95, in Kane and Donaldson's edition of the *B Text*.
4. Potter, p.105.
5. In exactly the same way, Magnificence is visited by Poverty and Adversity and reduced to wearing rags immediately prior to the entrance of Despair and Mischief.
6. See IV.iii. 64–6 and V.ii. 216–8, in vol.III of Dekker's *Dramatic Works*.
7. As well as Massinger's tendency (shared with other Jacobeans) to Christianise pagan philosophy, the peculiar circumstances of this particular play's origins may explain the more obviously anachronistic elements. The play, as we have it, is a complete rewrite of an earlier version, set in the sixteenth century, which was refused a licence by Sir Henry Herbert 'because itt did contain dangerous matter, as the deposing of Sebastian king of Portugal, by Philip the [Second,] and ther being a peace sworen twixte the kings of England and Spayne.' See the Introduction to the play in the Edwards and Gibson edition, IV, 293.
8. Another echo of *Doctor Faustus* is the way in which the temptation of despair is immediately succeeded by the temptation of beauty. Unlike Faustus, who succumbs to the spirit in the shape of Helen of Troy, Antiochus perceives the falsity of the beautiful courtesan sent to him by the Romans.
9. *The White Devil*, I.i. 49–51.
10. Quoted in Frye, p.119.
11. Burton, 3, 4, 2, 6, p.735.
12. Tyndale, 'The Obedience of a Christian Man', *Doctrinal Treatises*, p.135.
13. Burton, *loc.cit*. There are several illustrations of this doctrine in Wither's *A Collection of Emblemes*. On p.17 (Ixvii) the illustration is of a piece of metal on an anvil, waiting to be hammered into shape. The head-couplet reads,

> *Till* God *hath wrought us to his Will,*
> *The* Hammer *we shall suffer still.*

The poem beneath continues,

> For, by *Afflictions*, man refined growes,
> And, (as the *Gold* prepared in the *Fire*)
> Receiveth such a *Forme* by wrongs and blowes,
> That hee becomes the *Jewell* we desire.

See also Emblems IIxlvi and IIIxxxvii.
14. Susan Snyder, 'The Left Hand of God', p.27.
15. Gordon Rupp, *The Righteousness of God*, p.282.
16. More, *A Dialogue of Comfort against Tribulation*, II 16, p. 146.

17. *Works*, II, 19.
18. Seneca, 'On Providence', *Moral Essays*, I, 41.
19. Potter, p.159. The appropriateness of the imaginary setting for a temptation to despair may be demonstrated by Horatio's fear that the Ghost will tempt Hamlet

> to the dreadful summit of the cliff
> That beetles o'er his base into the sea, ...
> The very place puts toys of desperation,
> Without more motive into every brain
> That looks so many fathoms to the sea
> And hears it roar beneath.
>
> (I.iv. 70–8)

20. When Techelles presents Agydas with '*a naked dagger*' in Part One of Marlowe's *Tamburlaine*, Agydas immediately realises that he is supposed to kill himself (although in this case suicide will be an honourable way out rather than an act of despair). See III.ii. 88 ff.
21. D.C. Gunby, '*The Duchess of Malfi*: A Theological Approach', p.190.
22. Ibid., p.192.
23. Montaigne, IIxiii, 'Of Judging of Others' Death', p.211. The likelihood of this being a source for Bosola's line is increased by the presence of two definite Webster borrowings in the same chapter.
24. This theme is touched on again by Bosola, in his role as tomb-maker. He tells the Duchess that Princes' images on their tombs 'are not carved with their eyes fixed upon the stars, but as their minds were wholly bent upon the world, the selfsame way they seem to turn their faces' (IV.ii. 159–62).
25. The precise significance of Bosola's appearance as 'the common bellman' is fully explained by J.R. Brown in the Revels Plays edition:

> In 1605, a charity was presented to the church of St Sepulchre near Newgate prison, to provide a *bellman* to make a speech outside the dungeon of condemned prisoners the night before their execution, and another the next morning as the cart conveying them to Tyburn was stayed outside the church; this was to 'put them in minde of their mortalitie' and so 'to awake their sleepie senses from securitie, to save their soules from perishing' (*London's Dove* (1612), C4ᵛ).
>
> (Note to IV.ii. 173)

The 'John Webster' who was one of the signatories to this bequest is now known to have been the dramatist's father.
26. Dominic Baker-Smith, 'Religion and John Webster', p.228.
27. D.C. Gunby, *art. cit.*, attempts it by claiming that Antonio's death is part of a criticism of the limitations of neo-Stoic philosophy. See pp.200–1.
28. R. Ornstein, *The Moral Vision of Jacobean Tragedy*, p.150.

CHAPTER 4

1. Donne, p.46.
2. Quoted by Robert H. West, in 'The Christianness of *Othello*', p.340.
3. Quoted by Susan Snyder in 'The Left Hand of God', p.34.
4. Donne, pp. 186–7. The Donatist Petilian went so far as to claim that Judas had died a martyr's death.
5. Irving Ribner, in his Introduction to the Revels Plays edition, p.lvii.
6. *The Works of Thomas Nashe*, I, 294.
7. William Perkins, *The Whole Treatise of the Cases of Conscience*, II, xv, 3, pp.431–2.
8. Subconsciously, St Francis of Assisi may have recognised the equivocal nature of an ascetic's death. The dying saint imagined 'he heard a voice saying: "Francis, there is no sinner in the world whom, if he be converted, God will not pardon; but he who kills himself by hard penances will find no mercy in eternity." He attributed the voice to the devil' (Lecky, II, 49).
9. In the second (and happier) ending of Woodes's *The Conflict of Conscience*, Philologus's death after fasting and lack of sleep is not regarded as suicide: 'And nowe the Lord, in mercy great hath easde him of his payne' (l.2424)
10. 'The Theme of Damnation in Shakespearean Tragedy', p.243 n.
11. Laurentius Grimaldus, *The Counsellor*, sig. M6^r.
12. Wilhelmina P. Frijlinck thought that the pathos of Act III scene vi was 'undeniably due to Fletcher's genius'. See the Introduction to her edition of the play, p.xci.
13. In fact, the historical Barnaveld (*sic*) did view his death in Christian rather than pagan terms. He claimed he was 'going to God by the shortest road' (the Frijlinck edn, p.cxliv).
14. The same paradox is present in *Sir John van Olden Barnavelt*. Although Leidenberch redeems himself and atones for his fault, our opinion of Barnavelt is lowered by his callous insistence on Leidenberch's death. This (unhistorical) insistence was thought by Thomas Locke (in the letter which tells of the play's performance) 'to be a point strayned'. The letter implies that even Barnavelt could not have sunk as low as that. (See the Frijlinck edn, p.cxliv.)
15. Interestingly enough, men who died in duels were treated by the Church authorities as if they were suicides. They could not expect a Christian burial:
    > No Churchmans prayer to comfort their last groanes,
    > No sacred s[o]d of earth to hide their bones;
    > But as their fury wrought them out of breath,
    > The Canon speaks them guiltie of their owne death.
    >   (*The Devil's Law Case*, II.iii. 94–7)
16. Ornstein, *The Moral Vision of Jacobean Tragedy*, p.176.
17. *Patterns in Shakespearean Tragedy*, pp.95–6.
18. Siegel, 'The Damnation of *Othello*', pp.1068–78, and idem.,

Shakespearean Tragedy and the Elizabethan Compromise, pp.119–41; Bethell, 'Shakespeare's Imagery: The Diabolic Images in *Othello*', pp.62–80.

19. 'The Damnation of Othello', p.1072 n.
20. See Naseeb Shaheen, '"Like the Base Judean"'; and Joan Ozark Holmer, 'Othello's Threnos'.
21. ˙Hooker, *Of the Laws of Ecclesiastical Polity*, II, 214–15.
22. 'Othello's Threnos'.
23. *A Short View of Tragedy*, in *Critical Works*, p.134. It is possible that there is a sarcastic, double-edged quality about Rymer's remark, similar to the concluding line of Surrey's 'Sardanapalus' sonnet ('Murdred hym selfe to shew some manfull dede').
24. *The Business of Criticism*, p.39 n.
25. *Religio Medici* II, 7, in *Works*, I, 80.

CHAPTER 5

1. Lecky, II, 316.
2. Donne, p.76.
3. Ibid, p.142.
4. *Of the Citie of God*, lxviii, p.31.
5. Donne, p.143.
6. Andrew Willet, *An Harmonie upon I Samuel*, xxxi, q.4, p.174.
7. Quotations from Shakespeare's poems are from the same source as quotations from the plays, *The Complete Pelican Shakespeare*.
8. Fedden, p.132.
9. Ian Donaldson, *The Rapes of Lucretia*, p.40. This book is an excellent account of the way different periods have reacted to and reshaped the Lucrece story.
10. Who turns out to be Alcestis, whose readiness to die for Admetus made her a 'kalender .../ To any woman that wol lover be' (ll.542–3 of the Prologue (*B Text*), p.365 of the *Complete Works*).
11. Montaigne, IIi, 'Of the Inconstancie of our Actions', p.166. It might be argued, of course, that Montaigne's story is not so much a piece of genuine reporting as part of the establishment of a counter-myth in which the importance of rape is minimised (cf. Donaldson, *The Rapes of Lucretia*, Ch.5, 'Joking About Rape: The Myth Inverted').
12. There are grounds for supposing that in an earlier draft of the play, she *did* poison herself. In the text as it stands, there is some confusion between her original plan and what actually happens. As she gives the King the sleeping draught she adds,

> Because I'le quench the flames of wild desire,
> I'le drink this off, let fire conquer love's fire.
>
> (III.ii. 58–9).

13. See Donaldson, pp.108–10.
14. See Anne Lancashire's Introduction to the Revels Plays edition, pp.43–4.
15. The incident is mentioned by E.P. Kuhl in 'Shakespeare's *Rape of Lucrece*', pp.359–60.
16. The phrase occurs in Holland's translation of Livy's version of the Appius and Virginia story. See Webster's *Complete Works*, ed. F.L. Lucas, III, 132.
17. And, once more, there is a political dimension to the situation. The suicide of his wife invests Antonio with the moral authority to assume power at the end of the play and, moreover, the means to do so (the lords who swore to avenge her death).
18. This is one of the points made in a very good article by Coppélia Kahn, who also notes that the detail of the blood dividing is not found in any of Shakespeare's possible sources. See 'The Rape in Shakespeare's *Lucrece*', pp.64–5.

CHAPTER 6

1. From Lorenzo de' Medici's commentary on his own sequence of love sonnets. Quoted by Edgar Wind in *Pagan Mysteries in the Renaissance*, p.157.
2. Ficino, *De Amore*, II.viii, quoted by Wind, p.161. Ficino is the only source for the Orphic attribution of *glukupikron*, which in fact derives from Sappho.
3. The wives, respectively, of Pompey, Brutus, Paetus, and Seneca. Paulina was resuscitated on Nero's orders after she had attempted to bleed herself to death like her husband.
4. Denis de Rougemont, *Passion and Society*, trans. Montgomery Belgion, p.44.
5. Ibid., p.207.
6. *Works*, II, 320. Note also Shakespeare's Sonnet 144, 'Two loves I have, of comfort and despair'.
7. R.M. Frye, *Shakespeare and Christian Doctrine*, p.26.
8. John Bishop, *Beautifull Blossomes*, fol.52^v.
9. Printed 1591–92. It is a revised version of *Gismond of Salerne* which had been written 25 years before by Wilmot and four others. The story is taken from Boccaccio's *Decameron*.
10. Leonora Leet Brodwin, *Elizabethan Love Tragedy*, p.43.
11. Paul N. Siegel, 'Christianity and the Religion of Love in *Romeo and Juliet*', p.372.
12. L.G. Salingar, 'The Decline of Tragedy', p.436.
13. Even if it were Fletcher who wrote this scene, as is claimed by Cyrus Hoy ('The Shares of Fletcher and his Collaborators in the Beaumont and Fletcher Canon (II)', p.145), it is still quite possible that it was Massinger's views on suicide which determined its form.
14. Siegel, *art. cit.*, p.372.

15. Some critics have nevertheless done so, and are mentioned by Siegel (p.371).
16. Denis de Rougemont, *Passion and Society*, p.191.
17. G. Wither, *A Collection of Emblemes*, Ixxxiii, p.33.
18. Jacques Ferrand, *Erotomania* [trans. E. Chilmead], p.97.
19. 'On Ophelia's Madness', p.248.
20. 'Perhaps the purest poetry to be found in the whole of Ford's writings' ('John Ford', *Selected Essays*, p.198).
21. Leonora Leet Brodwin, *Elizabethan Love Tragedy*, p.144.
22. Ibid., p.146.
23. *The Anatomie of Mortalitie*, p.273.
24. 'Of Death', *Essays*, I, 4–5.
25. Fredson Bowers, *Elizabethan Revenge Tragedy*, p.215.
26. 'Religious Despair in Medieval Literature and Art', p.241.
27. *The Theatre of Gods Judgements*, IIxii, p.313.
28. *Not Wisely but too Well* (1957), quoted by Kenneth Muir in 'Elizabeth I, Jodelle, and Cleopatra', p.198.
29. *Art. cit.*
30. J.H. Hanford, 'Suicide in the Plays of Shakespeare', p.389.
31. Paul Cantor, *Shakespeare's Rome: Republic and Empire*, p.180.

CHAPTER 7

1. *Shakespeare's Roman Plays: The Function of Imagery in the Drama*, p.209.
2. The necrophilic aspect is rather more evident in the scene from *Bonduca*:

> What do I ail, i' th' name of heaven? I did but see her,
> And see her die: she stinks by this time strongly,
> Abominably stinks: she was a woman,
> A thing I never car'd for: but to die so,
> So confidently, bravely, strongly; O the devil,
> I have the bots, ...
>> the plain bots;
> A —— upon the bots, the love-bots.
>> (V.ii. 1–10)

3. Montaigne, by contrast, chooses to see the deaths of Brutus and Cassius not as an assertion of political freedom but as an abdication of political responsibility: 'Brutus and Cassius, by reason of the down-fall and rashnesse, wherewith before due time and occasion they killed themselves; did utterly lose the reliques of the Roman libertie, whereof they were protectors (IIiii, p.176).
4. C.H. Herford and P. and E. Simpson, *Ben Jonson*, II, 14.
5. *The Moral Philosophie of the Stoicks*, trans. T.J.[ames]., p.141.
6. 'Seneca in Elizabethan Translation', in *Selected Essays*, p.72.

7. W. Farnham, *The Medieval Heritage of Elizabethan Tragedy*, p.18.
8. Peter Ure, 'Chapman's Tragedies', in *Jacobean Theatre*, p.242.
9. J. Wieler, *George Chapman—the Effect of Stoicism upon his Tragedies*, p.163.
10. Montaigne, Ixxxvi, p.106.
11. There is an interesting account of changing views of Cato in the last chapter of Ian Donaldson, *The Rapes of Lucretia*.
12. William Whitaker, *A Disputation on Holy Scripture Against the Papists*, trans. William Fitzgerald, p.95.
13. David Fishel, 'The Image of Rome in Elizabethan and Jacobean Drama', pp.154–5. I am indebted at several points to Fishel's analysis of *Caesar and Pompey*.
14. Preface to *The Odyssey*, *Chapman's Homer*, II, 4.
15. G.K. Hunter's Introduction to his edition of *Antonio and Mellida*, p.xviii.
16. Ibid., p.xii.
17. There is a very similar scene in Massinger's *The Maid of Honour*, when the imprisoned Bertoldo is discovered *'with a small booke, in fetters'* (IV.iii). After making the same point as Antonio, Bertoldo unfairly calls Seneca's suicide a betrayal of his principles ('straight the armour/ Of his so boasted fortitude, fel off' (IV.iii. 19–20)), before throwing the book away.
18. M. Higgins, 'The Convention of the Stoic Hero as Handled by Marston', p.340.
19. In Plutarch (and in Amyot's French translation) there is no direct contradiction since it is clear that Brutus's opinion that suicide is 'cowardly and vile' was something he believed when young and inexperienced but does so no longer. North's translation of the relevant passage begins as follows: '"Being yet but a young man and not over greatly experienced in the world, I trust (I know not how) a certain rule of philosophy by the which I did greatly blame and reprove Cato for killing of himself ..."' (*Shakespeare's Plutarch*, ed. T.J.B. Spencer, p.155). 'I trust' sounds like Brutus's current opinion but is in fact a shortened form of the past tense, equivalent to 'trusted'. Shakespeare may have been misled by North's ambiguous grammar, or may simply have preferred the sharper sense of self-contradiction as fitting in well with his general conception of Brutus.
20. '"Division 'tween Our Souls": Shakespeare's Stoic Brutus', p.177.
21. *Shakespeare's Plutarch*, p.103.
22. Ibid.
23. For a recent summary of the arguments for and against the idea that Shakespeare revised this scene and intended to delete one of Brutus's two reactions, see Thomas Clayton, '"Should Brutus Never Taste of Portia's Death but Once?" Text and Performance in *Julius Caesar*'. Clayton's conclusion, with which I am in full agreement, is that the two reactions make perfectly good dramatic and psychological sense.
24. Walter C. Foreman, *The Music of the Close*, p.52.

CHAPTER 8

1. The Porter's 'farmer that hanged himself on th'expectation of plenty' seems to have been one of these 'types'. He appears as a fully-fledged dramatic character in Jonson's *Every Man out of his Humour* (III.vii. and viii), when Sordido, who has hoarded grain in the hope of a bad harvest, tries to hang himself when good weather looks like causing an abundance and hence lowering the price. The notes to the Herford and Simpson edition list numerous references to such an improbable figure, to which I can add a further one in Thomas Tuke, *A Discourse of Death*, p.29.
2. *An Harmonie upon II Samuel*, p. 12.
3. Burton, 1, 4, 1, p.286.
4. *Elizabethan Revenge Tragedy*, p.40.
5. See Chapter 1, note 93, above.
6. See Michael MacDonald, 'The Inner Side of Wisdom: Suicide in Early Modern England', pp.568-9. The details of these and other similar cases come from the records of Star Chamber suits designed to recover from the heirs of alleged suicides goods forfeit to the Crown.
7. F.G. Emmison, *Elizabethan Life: Morals and the Church Courts*, p.35.
8. MacDonald, 'The Inner Side of Wisdom', p.569.
9. Quoted by C. Bridenbaugh, in *Vexed and Troubled Englishmen 1590-1642*, p.267.
10. Written by Francis Osborne long after the event, and quoted by Stephen Greenblatt in *Sir Walter Ralegh*, p.xi.
11. Robert Grudin, *Mighty Opposites*, pp.14-15.
12. See especially Chapter 10 of *Radical Tragedy*, 'Subjectivity and Social Process'.

Bibliography

I. EDITIONS OF PLAYS USED FOR QUOTATION

Anon., *Caesar's Revenge* (*The Tragedy of Caesar and Pompey*), ed. F.S. Boas (The Malone Society Reprints: Oxford, 1911).

Anon., *The Fatal Marriage; or, A Second Lucretia*, ed. S. Brigid Younghughes and Harold Jenkins (The Malone Society Reprints: Oxford, 1958/59).

Anon., *Lust's Dominion*, in vol.IV of *The Dramatic Works of Thomas Dekker*, ed. Fredson T. Bowers, 4 vols. (Cambridge University Press: Cambridge, 1953-61).

Anon., *Nero*, in *Nero and Other Plays*, ed. Herbert P. Horne, The Mermaid Series (T. Fisher Unwin: London [1888]).

Anon. [Thomas Middleton?], *The Revenger's Tragedy* (attributed to Tourneur), ed. R.A. Foakes, The Revels Plays (Methuen: London, 1966).

Anon. [Thomas Middleton?], *The Second Maiden's Tragedy*, ed. Anne Lancashire, The Revels Plays (Manchester University Press: Manchester, 1978).

Anon. [Thomas Kyd?], *Soliman and Perseda*, in *The Works of Thomas Kyd*, ed. F.S. Boas (Clarendon Press: Oxford, 1901; rev. edn 1955).

Anon., *The True Tragedy of Richard the Third*, ed. W.W. Greg (The Malone Society Reprints: Oxford, 1929).

Barnes, Barnabe, *The Devil's Charter*, ed. R.B. McKerrow, *Materialien*, VI (Louvain, 1904).

Beaumont, Francis and John Fletcher, *The Dramatic Works in the Beaumont and Fletcher Canon*, gen. ed. Fredson T. Bowers, vols.I-V (Cambridge University Press: Cambridge, 1966-).

——, *The Works of Francis Beaumont and John Fletcher*, ed. Arnold Glover and A.R. Waller, 10 vols. (Cambridge University Press: Cambridge, 1905-10).

B[ower], R[ichard], *Apius and Virginia*, ed. R.B. McKerrow and W.W. Greg (The Malone Society Reprints: Oxford, 1911).

Chapman, George, *The Plays of George Chapman: The Tragedies*, ed. T.M. Parrott (Routledge: London, 1910).

——, *Bussy D'Ambois*, ed. Nicholas Brooke, The Revels Plays (Methuen: London, 1964).

Dekker, Thomas, *The Dramatic Works of Thomas Dekker*, ed. Fredson T. Bowers, 4 vols. (Cambridge University Press: Cambridge, 1953-61).

Fletcher, John and Philip Massinger, *The Tragedy of Sir John van Olden Barnavelt*, ed. Wilhelmina P. Frijlinck (H.G. van Dorssen: Amsterdam, 1922).

Ford, John, *The Broken Heart*, ed. T.J. B. Spencer, The Revels Plays (Manchester University Press: Manchester, 1980).

——, *The Lover's Melancholy and Love's Sacrifice*, ed. S.P. Sherman, *Materialien*, XXIII (Louvain, 1908).

Heywood, Thomas, *The Dramatic Works of Thomas Heywood* [ed. R.H. Shepherd], 6 vols. (J. Pearson: London, 1874).

——, *A Woman Killed with Kindness*, ed. R.W. van Fossen, The Revels Plays (Methuen: London, 1961).

Jonson, Ben, *Ben Jonson*, ed. C.H. Herford and Percy and Evelyn Simpson, 11 vols. (Clarendon Press: Oxford, 1925-52).

Kyd, Thomas, *The Spanish Tragedy*, ed. Philip Edwards, The Revels Plays (Methuen: London, 1959).

Marlowe, Christopher, *The Complete Works of Christopher Marlowe*, ed. Fredson T. Bowers, 2 vols. (Cambridge University Press: Cambridge, 1973).

——, *Doctor Faustus*, ed. John D. Jump, The Revels Plays (Methuen: London, 1962).

Marston, John, *The Plays of John Marston*, ed. H. Harvey Wood, 3 vols. (Oliver & Boyd: Edinburgh and London, 1934-39).

——, *Antonio and Mellida*, ed. G.K. Hunter, Regent's Renaissance Drama Series (Arnold: London, 1965).

——, *Antonio's Revenge*, ed. W. Reavley Gair, The Revels Plays (Manchester University Press: Manchester, 1978).

——, *The Malcontent*, ed. G.K. Hunter, The Revels Plays (Methuen: London, 1975).

Massinger, Philip, *The Plays and Poems of Philip Massinger*, ed. Philip Edwards and Colin Gibson, 5 vols (Clarendon Press: Oxford, 1976).

Middleton, Thomas, *The Works of Middleton*, ed. A.H. Bullen, 8 vols. (John Nimmo: London, 1885-86).

——, *The Changeling*, ed. N.W. Bawcutt, The Revels Plays (Methuen: London, 1958; reprinted with adds., 1961).

——, *Women Beware Women*, ed. J.R. Mulryne, The Revels Plays (Methuen: London, 1975).

Munday, Anthony and Henry Chettle, *The Death of Robert Earl of Huntingdon*, ed. John C. Meagher (The Malone Society Reprints: Oxford, 1965/67).

Sampson, William, *The Vow Breaker*, ed. Hans Wallrath, *Materialien*, XLII (Louvain, 1914; reprinted Vaduz, 1963).

Shakespeare, William, *The Complete Pelican Shakespeare*, gen. ed. Alfred Harbage, rev. edn. (Penguin Books: Baltimore/Allen Lane: London, 1969).

Tourneur, Cyril, *The Atheist's Tragedy*, ed. Irving Ribner, The Revels Plays (Methuen: London, 1964).

Webster, John, *The Complete Works of John Webster*, ed. F.L. Lucas, 4 vols. (Chatto & Windus: London, 1927).

——, *The Duchess of Malfi*, ed. J.R. Brown, The Revels Plays (Methuen: London, 1964).

——, *The White Devil*, ed. J. R. Brown, The Revels Plays, 2nd edn (Methuen: London, 1966).

Wilmot, Robert, *The Tragedy of Tancred and Gismund*, ed. W.W. Greg (The Malone Society Reprints: Oxford, 1914).

Woodes, Nathaniel, *The Conflict of Conscience*, ed. Herbert Davis and F.P. Wilson (The Malone Society Reprints: Oxford, 1952).

II. OTHER PRIMARY SOURCES

Aquinas, St Thomas, *Summa Theologiae* [trans. and ed. T. Gilby *et al.*], 61 vols. (Blackfriars: London, [1963]–81).

Aristotle, *Nicomachean Ethics*, trans. H. Rackham, The Loeb Classical Library, rev. edn (Heinemann: London, 1934; reprinted 1968).

Aubrey, John, *Aubrey's Brief Lives*, ed. Oliver Lawson Dick, 3rd edn (Secker & Warburg: London, 1958).

Augustine, St, *Of the Citie of God*, trans. J[ohn] H[ealey], (George Eld: London, 1610).

Bacon, Francis, *Bacon's Essays*, ed. Edwin A. Abbott, 2 vols. (Longmans: London, 1876).

Beard, Thomas, *The Theatre of Gods Judgements*, 2nd edn (Adam Islip: London, 1612).

Bishop, John, *Beautifull Blossomes* (Henrie Cockyn: London, 1577).

Bolton, Robert, *Instructions for a Right Comforting Afflicted Consciences*, 2nd edn (T. Weaver: London, 1635).

Browne, Thomas, *Works*, ed. Geoffrey Keynes, 4 vols. (Faber: London, 1928).

Bryskett, Lodovick, *A Discourse of Civill Life* (William Apsley: London, 1606).

Burton, Robert, *The Anatomy of Melancholy*, 6th edn (1651–52), reprinted with an account of the author (Chatto & Windus: London, 1883).

Caesarius of Heisterbach, *The Dialogue on Miracles*, trans. H. von E. Scott and C.C. Swinton Bland, 2 vols. (Routledge: London, 1929).

Calvin, John, *Institutes*, trans. Henry Beveridge, 2 vols. (Clarke: London, 1949).

Chapman, George, *Chapman's Homer*, ed. Allardyce Nicoll, 2 vols. (Routledge: London, 1957).

Charron, Pierre, *Of Wisdome Three Bookes*, trans. S. Lennard, (Edward Blount and Will Apsley: London [1608]).

Chaucer, Geoffrey, *Complete Works*, ed. W.W. Skeat (Clarendon Press: Oxford, 1912; reprinted 1967).

Copley, Antony, *A Fig for Fortune*, reprinted for the Spenser Society (Manchester, 1883).

[Denny, Sir William], *Pelecanicidium; or, The Christian Adviser against Self-Murder* (Thomas Hucklescott: London, 1653).

Donne, John, *Biathanatos*, ed. Michael Rudick and M. Pabst Battin (Garland: New York and London, 1982).

——, *Paradoxes and Problems*, ed. Helen Peters (Clarendon Press: Oxford, 1980).

——, *Pseudo-Martyr*, (Walter Burre: London, 1610).

Du Bartas, Guillaume, *The Divine Weeks and Works*, trans. Joshua Sylvester, ed. Susan Snyder, 2 vols. (Clarendon Press: Oxford, 1979).

Du Vair, Guillaume, *The Moral Philosophie of the Stoicks*, trans. T.J.[ames], (T. Man: London, 1598).

Eccles, Mark (ed.), *The Macro Plays*, Early English Text Society (Oxford University Press: London, 1969).

Ferrand, Jacques, *Erotomania* [trans. E. Chilmead] (L. Lichfield: Oxford, 1640).

Foxe, John, *Acts and Monuments* (The Book of Martyrs), 4th edn (John Day: London, 1583).

Goulart, I. [or rather, S.], *Admirable and Memorable Histories*, trans. E. Grimeston (G. Slel: London, 1607).

Greville, Sir Fulke, *The Life of Sir Philip Sidney*, ed. Nowell Smith (Clarendon Press: Oxford, 1907).

Grimaldus, Laurentius, *The Counsellor* (Richard Bradocke: London, 1598).

Hooker, Richard, *Of the Laws of Ecclesiastical Polity*, ed. J. Keble, rev.

R.W. Church and F. Paget, 3 vols. (Clarendon Press: Oxford, 1888).

Langland, William, *Piers Plowman: The B Version*, ed. George Kane and E. Talbot Donaldson (Athlone Press: London, 1975).

Lipsius, Justus, *Two Bookes of Constancie*, trans. J. Stradling (R. Johnes: London, 1595).

Montaigne, Michel de, *The Essayes of Michael Lord of Montaigne* trans. John Florio, ed. Henry Morley (Routledge: London, 1885).

More, Sir Thomas, *A Dialogue of Comfort against Tribulation*, ed. Louis L. Martz and Frank Manley, vol.XII of the Yale edn of *The Complete Works* (Yale University Press: New Haven and London, 1976).

——, *Utopia*, ed. Edward Surtz and J.H. Hexter, vol. IV of the Yale edn (Yale University Press: New Haven and London, 1965).

Nashe, Thomas, *The Works of Thomas Nashe*, ed. R.B. McKerrow, 5 vols. (1904–10), rev. F.P. Wilson (Blackwell: Oxford, 1958).

Perkins, William, *The Whole Treatise of the Cases of Conscience* (T. Pickering: Cambridge, 1606).

Plato, *Phaedo*, trans. David Gallop (Clarendon Press: Oxford, 1975).

Plutarch, *The Philosophie, Commonlie Called, the Morals*, trans. Philemon Holland (A. Hatfield: London, 1603).

——, *Shakespeare's Plutarch*, ed. T.J.B. Spencer (Penguin: Harmondsworth, 1964).

Rymer, Thomas, *The Critical Works*, ed. Curt. A. Zimansky (Yale University Press: New Haven, 1956).

Seneca, Lucius Annaeus, *Ad Lucilium Epistulae Morales*, trans. R.M. Gummere, The Loeb Classical Library, 3 vols. (Heinemann: London, 1917–25).

——, *Moral Essays*, trans. J.W. Basore, The Loeb Classical Library, 3 vols. (Heinemann: London, 1928–35).

——, *Seneca His Tenne Tragedies*, ed. T. Newton, introd. T.S. Eliot, The Tudor Translations, 2 vols. (Constable: London, 1927).

Sidney, Sir Philip, *Arcadia*, ed. Maurice Evans (Penguin: Harmondsworth, 1977).

Skelton, John, *Magnificence*, ed. Paula Neuss, The Revels Plays (Manchester University Press: Manchester, 1980).

Spenser, Edmund, *Poetical Works*, ed. J.C. Smith and E. de Selincourt (Oxford University Press: London, 1912; reprinted 1969).

Strode, George, *The Anatomie of Mortalitie* (London, 1618).

Surrey, Henry Howard, Earl of, *Poems*, ed. Emrys Jones (Clarendon Press: Oxford, 1964).

Sym, John, *Life's Preservative against Self-Killing* (London, 1637).

Tuke, Thomas, *A Discourse of Death* (G. Norton: London, 1613).

Tyndale, William, *Doctrinal Treatises*, ed. Henry Walter for the Parker Society (Cambridge University Press: Cambridge, 1848).

Vaughan, William, *The Golden Grove*, 2nd edn (E. Stafford: London, 1608).

Whetstone, George, *The Honorable Reputation of a Souldier* (London, 1585).

Whitaker, William, *A Disputation on Holy Scripture Against the Papists*, trans. William Fitzgerald for the Parker Society (Cambridge University Press: Cambridge, 1849).

Willet, Andrew, *An Harmonie upon the First Booke of Samuel* (Cambridge, 1614).

——, *An Harmonie upon the Second Booke of Samuel* (Cambridge, 1614).

Willymat, William, *Physicke to Cure the Most Dangerous Disease of Desperation*, 2nd edn (R. Boulton: London, 1605).

Wither, George, *Abuses Stript and Whipt* (F. Burton: London, 1613).

——, *A Collection of Emblemes, Ancient and Moderne*, facsimile of 1635 edn (University of South Carolina Press: Columbia, South Carolina, 1975).

III.   SECONDARY SOURCES

Allen, D.C., 'Donne's Suicides', *Modern Language Notes*, LVI (1941), 129–33.

——, 'Some Observations on *The Rape of Lucrece*', *Shakespeare Survey*, XV (1962), 89–98.

Altman, Joel B., *The Tudor Play of Mind: Rhetorical Inquiry and the Development of Elizabethan Drama* (University of California Press: Berkeley, Los Angeles, and London, 1978).

Alvarez, Alfred, *The Savage God: A Study of Suicide* (Weidenfeld & Nicolson: London, 1971).

Ariès, Philippe, *Western Attitudes Towards Death*, trans. P.M. Ranum (Johns Hopkins University Press: Baltimore and London, 1974).

Babb, Lawrence, *The Elizabethan Malady: A Study of Melancholia in English Literature from 1580 to 1642* (Michigan State College Press: East Lansing, Mich., 1951).

Bacon, Wallace A., 'The Suicide of Antony', *Shakespeare Association Bulletin*, XXIV (1949), 193–202.

Baker-Smith, Dominic, 'Religion and John Webster' in *John Webster*, ed. Brian Morris (Benn: London, 1970), pp.207–28.

Battin, M. Pabst and David J. Mayo (eds.), *Suicide: The Philosophical Issues* (Peter Owen: London, 1981).

Bellamy, John, *Crime and Public Order in the Later Middle Ages* (Routledge: London, 1973).

Belsey, Catherine, 'The Case of Hamlet's Conscience', *Studies in Philology*, LXXVI (1979), 127–48.

Bethell, S.L., 'Shakespeare's Imagery: The Diabolic Images in *Othello*', *Shakespeare Survey*, V (1952), 62–80.

Black, James, 'King Lear: Art Upside Down', *Shakespeare Survey*, XXXIII (1980), 35–42.

Borges, Jorge Luis, *Other Inquisitions*, trans. Ruth L.C. Simms (University of Texas Press: Austin, Texas, 1964).

Bowers, Fredson T., *Elizabethan Revenge Tragedy 1587–1642* (Princeton University Press: Princeton, N.J., 1940; reprinted by Peter Smith: Gloucester, Mass., 1959).

Bradbrook, Muriel C., *Themes and Conventions of Elizabethan Tragedy* (Cambridge University Press: Cambridge, 1935; reprinted 1952).

Bridenbaugh, C., *Vexed and Troubled Englishmen 1590–1642* (Clarendon Press: Oxford, 1968).

Brodwin, Leonora Leet, *Elizabethan Love Tragedy 1587–1625* (New York University Press: New York, 1971/London University Press: London, 1972).

Brooke, Rupert, *John Webster and the Elizabethan Drama* (Sidgwick & Jackson: London, 1916).

Brower, Reuben A., *Hero and Saint: Shakespeare and the Graeco-Roman Heroic Tradition* (Clarendon Press: Oxford, 1971).

Brown, J.R. and Bernard Harris (eds.), *Jacobean Theatre*, Stratford-upon-Avon Studies, I (Arnold: London, 1960; reprinted with corrections, 1965).

Camden, Carroll, 'On Ophelia's Madness', *Shakespeare Quarterly*, XV (1964), 247–55.

Campbell, Lily B., '*Doctor Faustus*: A Case of Conscience', *Publications of the Modern Language Association*, LXVII (1952), 219–39.

——, *Shakespeare's Tragic Heroes: Slaves of Passion* (Cambridge University Press: Cambridge, 1930; reprinted by Methuen: London, 1962).

Cantor, Paul A., *Shakespeare's Rome: Republic and Empire* (Cornell University Press: Ithaca and London, 1976).

Carey, John, *John Donne: Life, Mind and Art* (Faber: London, 1981).

Charlton, H.B., *The Senecan Tradition in Renaissance Tragedy* (Publications of the University of Manchester: Manchester, 1946).

Charney, Maurice, *Shakespeare's Roman Plays: The Function of Imagery in the Drama* (Harvard University Press: Cambridge, Mass., 1961).

Clayton, Thomas, '"Should Brutus Never Taste of Portia's Death but Once?" Text and Performance in *Julius Caesar*', *Studies in English Literature*, XXIII (1983), 237–55.

Colie, Rosalie L., *Paradoxia Epidemica: The Renaissance Tradition of Paradox* (Princeton University Press: Princeton, N.J., 1966).

Collmer, Robert G., 'Donne and Charron', *English Studies*, XLVI (1965), 482–8.

Cunningham, Dolora G., 'Macbeth: The Tragedy of the Hardened Heart', *Shakespeare Quarterly*, XIV (1963), 39–47.

Doebler, Bettie Anne, '"Dispaire and Dye": The Ultimate Temptation of Richard III', *Shakespeare Studies*, VII (1974), 75–85.

Dollimore, Jonathan, *Radical Tragedy: Religion, Ideology and Power in the Drama of Shakespeare and his Contemporaries* (Harvester: Brighton, 1984).

Donaldson, Ian, *The Rapes of Lucretia: A Myth and its Transformations* (Clarendon Press: Oxford, 1982).

Dublin, Louis and Bessie Bunzel, *To Be or Not to Be: A Study of Suicide* (Smith & Haas: New York, 1933).

Eliot, T.S., *Selected Essays*, 3rd edn (Faber: London, 1951; reprinted 1969).

Ellis-Fermor, Una, *The Jacobean Drama*, 4th edn rev. (Methuen: London, 1958).

Emmison, F.G., *Elizabethan Life: Morals and the Church Courts* (Essex County Council: Chelmsford, 1973).

Empson, William, *Some Versions of Pastoral* (Chatto & Windus: London, 1935; reprinted by Penguin with Chatto & Windus: London, 1966).

Faber, M.D., 'Shakespeare's Suicides: Some Historic, Dramatic, and Psychological Reflections', in *Essays in Self-Destruction*, ed. Edwin S. Shneidman (Science House: New York, 1967), pp.30–58.

Farnham, Willard, *The Medieval Heritage of Elizabethan Tragedy* (University of California Press: Berkeley, 1936; reprinted with corrections by Blackwell: Oxford, 1956).

Fedden, Henry Romilly, *Suicide: A Social and Historical Study* (Peter Davies: London, 1938).

Fetrow, Fred M., 'Chapman's Stoic Hero in *The Revenge of Bussy D'Ambois*', *Studies in English Literature*, XIX (1979), 229–37.

Fishel, David, 'The Image of Rome in Elizabethan and Jacobean Drama', unpub. M.Litt. thesis (Oxford University, 1978).

Forbes, T.R., *Chronicle from Aldgate: Life and Death in Shakespeare's London* (Yale University Press: New Haven and London, 1971).

Foreman, Walter C., Jr, *The Music of the Close: The Final Scenes of Shakespeare's Tragedies* (Kentucky University Press: Kentucky, 1978).

Frye, R.M., *The Renaissance 'Hamlet': Issues and Responses in 1600* (Princeton University Press: Princeton, N.J., 1984).

——, *Shakespeare and Christian Doctrine* (Princeton University Press: Princeton, N.J./ Oxford University Press: London, 1963).

Gardner, Helen, *The Business of Criticism* (Clarendon Press: Oxford, 1959).

——, 'Milton's Satan and the Theme of Damnation in Elizabethan Tragedy', *English Studies*, n.s. I (1948), 46–66.

——, *Religion and Literature* (Faber: London, 1971).

Greaves, Richard, *Society and Religion in Elizabethan England* (University of Minnesota Press: Minneapolis, 1981).

Green, Paul D., 'Doors to the House of Death: The Treatment of Suicide in Sidney's *Arcadia*', *Sixteenth Century Journal*, X (1979), 17–27.

——, 'Suicide, Martyrdom and Thomas More', *Studies in the Renaissance*, XIX (1972), 135–55.

——, 'Theme and Structure in Fletcher's *Bonduca*', *Studies in English Literature*, XXII (1982), 305–16.

Greenblatt, Stephen J., *Sir Walter Ralegh: The Renaissance Man and His Roles* (Yale University Press: New Haven and London, 1973).

Grudin, Robert, *Mighty Opposites: Shakespeare and Renaissance Contrariety* (University of California Press: Berkeley, Los Angeles, and London, 1979).

Gunby, D.C., '*The Duchess of Malfi*: A Theological Approach', in *John Webster*, ed. Brian Morris (Benn: London, 1970), pp.181–204.

Hair, P.E.H., 'Deaths from Violence in Britain: A Tentative Secular Survey', *Population Studies*, XXV, 1 (1971), 5–24.

——, 'A Note on the Incidence of Tudor Suicide', *Local Population Studies*, V (1970), 36–43.

Hanford, J.H., 'Suicide in the Plays of Shakespeare', *Publications of the Modern Language Association*, XXVII (1912), 380–98.

Hastings, James (ed.), *Encyclopaedia of Religion and Ethics*, 12 vols. (Clark: Edinburgh, 1908–21).

Hibbard, G.R., 'The Early Seventeenth Century and the Tragic View of Life', *Renaissance and Modern Studies*, V (1961), 5–28.

Higgins, M., 'The Convention of the Stoic Hero as Handled by Marston', *Modern Language Review*, XXXIX (1944), 338–46.

Holmer, Joan Ozark, 'Othello's Threnos', *Shakespeare Studies*, XIII (1980), 145–67.

Hoy, Cyrus, 'The Shares of Fletcher and his Collaborators in the Beaumont and Fletcher Canon', *Studies in Bibliography*, VIII–XV (1956–62).

Ide, Richard S., *Possessed with Greatness: The Heroic Tragedies of Chapman and Shakespeare* (Scolar: London, 1980).

Jenkins, Harold (ed.), Introduction and Notes to the Arden *Hamlet* (Methuen: London and New York, 1982).

Kahn, Coppélia, 'The Rape in Shakespeare's *Lucrece*', *Shakespeare Studies*, IX (1976), 45–72.

Kistner, A.L. and M.K., 'The Senecan Background of Despair in *The Spanish Tragedy* and *Titus Andronicus*', *Shakespeare Studies*, VII (1974), 1–9.

Kuhl, E.P., 'Shakespeare's *Rape of Lucrece*', *Philological Quarterly*, XX (1941), 352–60.

Lacey, Robert, *Sir Walter Ralegh* (Weidenfeld & Nicolson: London, 1973).

Latham, Agnes M.C., 'Sir Walter Ralegh's Farewell Letter to his Wife in 1603: A Question of Authenticity', *Essays and Studies*, XXV (1939), 39–58.

Lecky, William E.H., *History of European Morals*, 2 vols., 3rd edn rev. (Longmans: London, 1877).

Leech, Clifford, *The John Fletcher Plays* (Chatto & Windus: London, 1962).

Lucas, F.L., *Seneca and Elizabethan Tragedy* (Cambridge University Press: Cambridge, 1922).

MacDonald, Michael, 'The Inner Side of Wisdom: Suicide in Early Modern England', *Psychological Medicine*, VII (1977), 565–82.

Margeson, J.M.R., *The Origins of English Tragedy* (Clarendon Press: Oxford, 1967).

McAlindon, T., *English Renaissance Tragedy* (Macmillan: London, 1985).

——, *Shakespeare and Decorum* (Macmillan: London, 1973).

Monaco, Marion, 'Racine and the Problem of Suicide', *Publications of the Modern Language Association*, LXX (1955), 441–54.

Muir, Kenneth, 'Elizabeth I, Jodelle, and Cleopatra', *Renaissance Drama*, n.s. II (1969), 197–206.

Myrick, K.O., 'The Theme of Damnation in Shakespearean Tragedy', *Studies in Philology*, XXXVII (1941), 221–45.

Noon, Georgia, 'On Suicide', *Journal of the History of Ideas*, XXXIX (1978), 371–86.

Ornstein, Robert, '*The Atheist's Tragedy* and Beard's Account of Marlowe's Death', *Notes and Queries* (July 1955), 284–5.

——, *The Moral Vision of Jacobean Tragedy* (University of Wisconsin Press: Madison, 1960).

Peat, Derek, '"And that's true too": *King Lear* and the Tension of Uncertainty', *Shakespeare Survey*, XXXIII (1980), 43–53.

Petronella, Vincent F., 'Hamlet's "To be or not to be" Soliloquy: Once More unto the Breach', *Studies in Philology*, LXXI (1974), 72–88.

Pollin, Burton R., 'Hamlet, a Successful Suicide', *Shakespeare Studies*, I (1965), 240–60.

Potter, Robert, *The English Morality Play* (Routledge: London and Boston, 1975).

Price, Hereward T., 'The Function of Imagery in Webster', *Publications of the Modern Language Association*, LXX (1955), 717–39.

Prosser, Eleanor, *Hamlet and Revenge*, 2nd edn (Stanford University Press: Stanford, Calif., 1971).

Rabkin, Norman, *Shakespeare and the Common Understanding* (The Free Press: New York/Collier-Macmillan: London, 1967).

Ribner, Irving, *Jacobean Tragedy: The Quest for Moral Order*, (Methuen: London, 1962).

——, *Patterns in Shakespearean Tragedy* (Methuen: London, 1960).

Rist, J.M., *Stoic Philosophy* (Cambridge University Press: Cambridge, 1969).

Roberts, D.R., 'The Death Wish of John Donne', *Publications of the Modern Language Association*, LXII (1947), 958–76.

Rossiter, A.P., *Angel with Horns, and other Shakespeare Lectures*, ed. G. Storey (Longmans: London, 1961).

Rougemont, Denis de, *Passion and Society*, trans. Montgomery Belgion, rev. and enlarged edn (Faber: London, 1956).

Rupp, Gordon, *The Righteousness of God* (Hodder & Stoughton: London, 1953).

Sacharoff, Mark, 'Suicide and Brutus' Philosophy in *Julius Caesar*', *Journal of the History of Ideas*, XXXIII (1972), 115–22.

Sachs, Arieh, 'Religious Despair in Medieval Literature and Art', *Medieval Studies*, XXVI (1964), 231–56.

——, 'The Religious Despair of Doctor Faustus', *Journal of English and Germanic Philology*, LXIII (1964), 625–47.

Salingar, L.G., 'The Decline of Tragedy', in vol.II of *The Pelican Guide to English Literature*, ed. Boris Ford, 7 vols. (Penguin: Harmondsworth, 1954–61; reprinted with revisions 1969), pp.429–40.

Shaheen, Naseeb, ' "Like the Base Judean" ', *Shakespeare Quarterly*, XXXI (1980), 93–5.

Shepherd, Simon, *Amazons and Warrior Women: Varieties of Feminism in Seventeenth-Century Drama* (Harvester: Brighton, 1981).

Siegel, Paul N., 'Christianity and the Religion of Love in *Romeo and Juliet*', *Shakespeare Quarterly*, XII (1961), 371–92.

——, 'The Damnation of Othello', *Publications of the Modern Language Association*, LXVIII (1953), 1068–78.

——, *Shakespearean Tragedy and the Elizabethan Compromise* (New

York University Press: New York, 1957).

Simmons, J.L., *Shakespeare's Pagan World: The Roman Tragedies* (Harvester: Brighton, 1974).

Simpson, Evelyn M., *A Study of the Prose Works of John Donne*, 2nd edn (Clarendon Press: Oxford, 1948).

Slights, Camille Wells, *The Casuistical Tradition in Shakespeare, Donne, Herbert, and Milton* (Princeton University Press: Princeton, N.J., 1981).

Snyder, Susan, 'The Left Hand of God: Despair in Medieval and Renaissance Tradition', *Studies in the Renaissance*, XII (1965), 18–59.

Spencer, Theodore, *Death and Elizabethan Tragedy* (Harvard University Press: Cambridge, Mass., 1936).

Sprott, S.E., *The English Debate on Suicide from Donne to Hume* (Open Court: La Salle, Ill., 1961).

Stachniewski, John, 'John Donne: The Despair of the "Holy Sonnets"', *English Literary History*, XLVIII (1981), 677–705.

Stilling, Roger, *Love and Death in Renaissance Tragedy* (Louisiana State University Press: Baton Rouge, Louisiana, 1976).

Sullivan, Ernest W., II (ed.), Introduction to his edition of Donne's *Biathanatos* (University of Delaware Press: Newark, 1984).

Toynbee, A.J. *et al.*, *Man's Concern with Death* (Hodder & Stoughton: London, 1968).

Vawter, Marvin L., '"Division 'tween Our Souls": Shakespeare's Stoic Brutus', *Shakespeare Studies*, VII (1974), 173–95.

Vyvyan, John, *The Shakespearean Ethic* (Chatto & Windus: London, 1959).

Waith, E.M., *The Herculean Hero: In Marlowe, Chapman, Shakespeare and Dryden* (Chatto & Windus: London, 1962).

——, *The Pattern of Tragicomedy in Beaumont and Fletcher* (Yale University Press: New Haven, 1952).

Walley, Harold R., '*The Rape of Lucrece* and Shakespearean Tragedy', *Publications of the Modern Language Association*, LXXVI (1961), 480–7.

Warner, Marina, *Alone of All her Sex: The Myth and the Cult of the Virgin Mary* (Weidenfeld & Nicolson: London, 1976).

Watson, Curtis Brown, *Shakespeare and the Renaissance Concept of Honor* (Princeton University Press: Princeton, N.J., 1960).

West, Robert H., 'The Christianness of Othello', *Shakespeare Quarterly*, XV (1964), 333–43.

Wieler, John W., *George Chapman—The Effect of Stoicism upon his Tragedies* (King's Crown Press: New York, 1949).

Wilson, F.P., *Elizabethan and Jacobean* (Clarendon Press: Oxford, 1945; reprinted 1969).

Wind, Edgar, *Pagan Mysteries in the Renaissance*, rev. and enlarged edn (Faber: London, 1968).

Wymer, Rowland, 'Lodovick Bryskett and Renaissance Attitudes to Suicide', *Notes and Queries* (December 1985), 480–2.

Index